Pr:

7 Secrets Guys Will Never Tell You

"This is an amazing book! *7 Secrets Guys Will Never Tell You* not only encourages girls like me to choose celibacy, but also to gain enough respect for ourselves that we command it from others. It reminds us that we are priceless, and should never settle when it comes to decisions about love, sex and relationships."

—Taylor Dortch, 16-year-old student

"I appreciate the fact that *7 Secrets Guys Will Never Tell You* isn't a male bashing book. It honestly and effectively depicts the 3 types of guys that girls should be aware of, from the player, to the good guy, to the best guy. I was amazed that the author knew so much about guys' mentality and behavior. It's obvious she has spent a lot of time talking with guys. This book gave me hope that us 'Best Guys' will not be placed on the back burner when girls consider relationship partners."

—Tyri Brown, 19-year-old soldier

"*7 Secrets Guys Will Never Tell You* was an amazing read. The stories in the book told by the teens themselves brought a real life perspective all girls need to hear. As a father to a beautiful 16-year-old daughter, I can definitely say this is a book every father would want his daughter to read immediately."

—Cliff Baskerville, Father of a teen daughter

"Honest, direct, and compassionate all in one. I wish I had read this book before every relationship, even in college. The truth written on these pages has the power to transform girls into ambitious, confident, and driven women who will know their worth."

—Gretchen Kaufman, 23-year-old graduate student

"This book really helped me to know my worth, even at age 35. If I had read this book as a teenager, it would've saved me much heartache and regrets. As a result of this book, I also feel more prepared to help my teenage son know his worth and understand the benefits of practicing self-control."

—Mia Carey, Mother of a teenage son

"Unfortunately, what girls don't know can hurt them—sometimes for life. With this life-changing book by Jackie Brewton, your teen will be able to see the blind spots before she dates and date wiser . . . and SAFER because of it. This is not a book—it's an intervention. I have seen first hand how this book will change lives."

—Dr. Alduan Tartt, Psychologist, Speaker, Media Personality, and Author of *The Ring Formula: How to be the Only One He EVER Needs*

"Honest, insightful and thought provoking!!! Jackie Brewton has done a REMARKABLE job in *7 Secrets Guys Will Never Tell You*, dispelling myths and exposing the truth when it comes to love, sex and relationships. This book is a MUST READ for every teenage girl, parent and youth leader."

—Nicole Steele, Author of *Priceless: A Girl's Guide to Uncovering the Beauty, Boldness & Brilliance Within*, Confidence Coach and Executive Director of Diamond In The Rough

"As one who mentors and speaks to young men daily, I believe this book gives young ladies a front row seat into the minds of young men, without them having to go through all of the tragic life experiences to get that seat. Read this book, and also share it with every young woman you know!"
—Chris Cannon, Author of *The Mystery of Manhood*

"I LOVED the book! Jackie Brewton's approach is unique. This is not the typical book that relies on scare tactics: unwanted pregnancies, STDs, etc. Rather, it uses the testimonies and admissions of teen guys and the flawed thinking of teen girls to reveal how engaging in teen sex is counterproductive to what a teen girl really searches for: love, acceptance, and (too often) her father's approval. This book will help many girls keep their lives on track and others to get back on track to a successful future. If I had one book that I could give to a teen daughter, *7 Secrets Guys Will Never Tell You* would be the book."
—Annette Pearson, Middle School teacher for 18 years

"*7 Secrets Guys Will Never Tell You* gives practical advice to assist young ladies in recognizing that they deserve the best relationship and not to settle for anything less. Jackie illustrates her points with tangible examples and clear analogies. She encourages young ladies that having high standards for themselves creates confidence, helping them value themselves apart from any relationship status."
—Christa Slyman, Relationship Educator and Mother of two teenagers

SECRETS GUYS WILL NEVER TELL YOU

A Teen Girl's Guide on Love, Sex, and Relationships

JACKIE BREWTON

Copyright © 2016 by Jackie Brewton
All Rights Reserved
Published by HLB Press
www.hlbpress.com

All rights reserved. No part of this book may be reproduced in any form or by any means, electronic or mechanical, including photocopying or recording, or by any information and storage retrieval system, without written permission of the publisher.

ISBN: 978-0-9973405-0-1 (paperback)
ISBN: 978-0-9973405-1-8 (ebook: ePub)
ISBN: 978-0-9973405-2-5 (ebook: Kindle / mobi)

Source for statistics on Pages 34, 57, 72, 114, and 143:
The National Campaign to Prevent Teen and Unplanned Pregnancy. (2010). *That's What He Said: What Guys Think About Sex, Love, Contraception, and Relationships.* Retrieved from http://thenationalcampaign.org/resource/thats-what-he-said

Printed in the U.S.A.

Book design by DesignForBooks.com

Contents

Acknowledgments vii

Introduction ix

    How do I know guys' secrets? ix
    Why write to girls? x
    What is this book **not** about? x
    The three types of girls who will read this book. xii
    The three types of guys we will
        discuss in this book. xiii
    How can you tell the difference? xvi

Secret 1: Sex doesn't equal love. 1

    How is love portrayed in our culture? 3
    What is love? 4
    How is love shown? 6
    If it's selfish, it's not love. 9
    Why settle for sex when you're
        looking for real love? 12
    Love Is almost never forever in high school. 14
    Chase your dreams, not relationships. 16
    Who should be your first love? 17
    Relationships are not a measure of your worth. 18
    Now that you know . . . 20

Secret 2: They'll tell you what you want to hear.   23

    Why do guys tell you what you want to hear?   24
    What's a common way guys lie to get sex?   31
    What are the common lines guys use?   34
    Why do girls believe the lies?   43
    Now that you know . . .   46

Secret 3: They won't respect you if you don't respect yourself.   49

    Respect earns respect.   50
    What is self-respect?   51
    How can a guy tell whether you respect yourself?   53
    The test   55
    How can you tell if a guy respects you?   59
    Why don't girls always demand respect?   69
    Respect—starting over   73
    Now that you know . . .   75

Secret 4: Sex changes things.   77

    What changes?   80
    Why the change?   81
    What happens as a result of the changed feelings/expectations?   91
    Is it you or the sex?   95
    One way to tell: The Thirty-Days test   96
    Now that you know . . .   98

Secret 5: They're not looking for a wife.   101

    Even when guys commit, how long do they expect the relationships to last?   103
    Are you dating your future husband or just your future ex?   105
    Does commitment equal marriage for guys?   107
    Why can't guys commit—or can they?   109

contents

Will sex make guys commit?   110
How can sex with a future ex complicate your life?   115
Why do guys look for different qualities in
    wives than girlfriends?   117
Now that you know . . .   120

Secret 6: They can't replace your father.   123

The benefits of an actively engaged father.   126
The most common consequences of fatherlessness.   130
So what's a girl to do?   135
Now that you know . . .   138

Secret 7: They will wait if you will.   139

False assumptions girls make about guys.   142
Why don't girls wait for sex?   148
What are the benefits of waiting?   157
Now that you know . . .   161

Conclusion   165

Acknowledgments

This book was truly a labor of love. You see, Language Arts was my least favorite class in school. But, as much as I hate writing, I love empowering teen girls like you because I know you're worth it.

I am grateful for several people who contributed to the completion of this book. Without them it would not have been possible.

First, thank you to my friend and copywriter/virtual assistant La Monica Smith, who came up with the title for the book, laid out the framework for each chapter, read many versions and provided edits and feedback countless times.

Second, a special thank you goes to my good friend Carol Wade, who spent a gazillion hours working on the book with me on the phone. I appreciate her challenging me to create and follow an outline and pushing me to think deeper about what the *real* issue was or what I was *really* trying to say. She's a great writer in her own right, and I'm blessed to have had her involved with this book. I'm sure I tested her patience many times over, but she hung in there until the end, and I owe her big time.

Third, thank you to my niece Morgan Brewton-Johnson, for reading the book from a teen girl's perspective and preventing me from sounding too old-fashioned. Her input/edits/rewrites certainly made for a much better book than it would have been without her expertise. She should have taken me up

acknowledgments

on my original idea of co-authoring this book since she contributed so much.

Finally, I couldn't have written this book if it weren't for what I learned from Mrs. Wanda Fowler, the best English teacher ever. I hope what I've written has made her proud.

I can't forget about all the students who wrote the anonymous letters scattered throughout the pages of this book. I appreciate their honesty and transparency.

Most importantly, thank you for taking your time to read my labor of love.

Introduction

What if I told you I hold the key to unlocking seven secrets guys keep, that if you knew them, would help you avoid heartache and heartbreak? What would you do with that information? Well, wonder no longer. You now hold the key to discovering what guys think about love, sex and relationships straight from their own mouths. This book will give you a rare glimpse inside their minds, and hopefully these secrets will help you evaluate your current and future relationships through a different lens.

How do I know guys' secrets?

Right now, you may be thinking, *how does this woman know anything about the secrets of teenage boys?* Well, let me introduce myself. I'm a motivational speaker and health educator. I've gained this "inside scoop" from fourteen years of experience listening to young men share their honest thoughts and feelings about sex, love and relationships during my classes. They've also written me thousands of letters throughout the years, sharing their feelings and behaviors. I'll share stories of my discussions and interactions with guys and girls, as well as excerpts from more than one hundred letters from both.

introduction

Why write to girls?

I decided to write my first book specifically for young ladies for a few reasons.

First, my heart breaks every time I hold a young lady in my arms who's crying uncontrollably after realizing the high price she has paid for a boy's attention. It pains me to read a letter from a young lady who has had twenty-five sexual partners by the age of sixteen. I'm saddened every time I encounter young women who tell me they wish they'd heard me earlier. My hope is this book will prevent more girls from having to say "if only."

Secondly, I've been observing some behavior from girls that has me scratching my head and asking myself, "When did young ladies lose their way?" I've seen such a shift over the fourteen years I've been speaking to students in how young ladies interact with each other and relate to guys. The level of disrespect they have for themselves and accept from guys is disheartening. Young women are getting attention from guys, but it's not the type of attention they want, and I hear the awful things young men say about them behind their backs. My goal is to help these young ladies regain their dignity and prevent other girls from losing theirs.

Finally, I know not every girl is able to pull up a ringside seat and hear directly from the guys in my classes, so I want to make sure girls who don't have this opportunity still have access to this important information.

What is this book *not* about?

Instead of sharing what you can expect to learn from this book, I'd like to make it clear what you *won't* read.

1. This isn't a book that will bash guys. I will make a lot of

introduction

generalized statements about guys throughout the book, but even then, I want to be clear that I'm not talking about *all* guys. The guys I *do* talk about aren't always trying to be manipulative or hold these secrets from you on purpose. Many times they just haven't thought deeply about their actions. Even though I'm letting you in on guys' secrets, this book is much more about *you* than it is about guys.

2. While much of this book is about sex, I won't try to scare you out of having it. Yes, I want you to know about the consequences you may suffer as a result of having sex, but that's not why I want you to make the decision not to. You should abstain from sex because you love and respect yourself enough to protect yourself, your future and your future family. With that said, even though I'm not trying to scare you, the truth is scary, and I'd rather you hear the ugly truth than believe a pretty lie.

3. I'm not trying to tell you how to live your life. I'm sure you have enough adults already trying to do that. I'm sharing this information so you'll never have to say, "I wish someone had told me."

> *... the truth is scary, and I'd rather you hear the ugly truth than believe a pretty lie.*

"Thanks for talking to the class, even though you told the girls our [the boys'] backdoor secrets. I guess they needed to know them. The sad thing is some girls still wouldn't believe what they heard; but they can't ever say they weren't told."

~HIGH SCHOOL GUY

You may not like a lot of what you read in this book. And as the young man stated in the quote above, you may not even believe what you read, but you'll never be able to say you didn't know.

The three types of girls who will read this book:

Type 1: She has already chosen to abstain from sex.

The first group includes the girls who wouldn't have sex whether they read this book or not because of their value system. They are the girls who are so busy focusing on their dreams and goals they don't have time for sex. These girls are saying yes to those bigger dreams like school, sports, and careers, so they feel empowered saying no to temporary things like sex that could get in their way.

Type 2: She has already chosen to have sex and will continue having sex.

On the opposite extreme are the girls who will still have sex even after reading this book. They are the girls who are convinced they can avoid any of the potential negative consequences that come from sex. They are also the girls who choose to learn the hard way. These are the girls who will touch a hot stove even after they've been warned, saying, "Just because you got burned doesn't mean I will."

Type 3: She is undecided about sex.

The middle group is the largest, and it includes the girls who are on the fence. They may be virgins, but only because the

introduction

opportunity to have sex hasn't presented itself. They don't have a plan, and therefore could be swayed in either direction. They may also be sexually active, but would stop having sex with the right information and motivation. This is the group I think will benefit most from this book.

If you are the girl who has already decided to abstain from sex even before picking up this book, I hope what you read will confirm that you've made the right choice. If you are the girl who will continue having sex even after you've read this book, I pray someone or something will be able to reach you before you suffer any major consequences. If you are the girl who is on the fence, hopefully this will be the deciding factor for you to make the best choice for your life.

The three types of guys we will discuss in this book:

Before I reveal the secrets, I have to establish not all guys are the same. I've found teenage guys normally fit into three categories. With each secret, I'll identify what each type of guy might be thinking.

Unfortunately, many girls aren't aware which type their boyfriends are until after they've been burned.

Type 1: The *Player*—He doesn't care about you and just wants sex.

This is the guy whose picture would be next to selfish in the dictionary. He has only one thing on his mind: sex. For him, sex is just another activity, like playing video games. And just like with video games, once he gets what he wants (i.e., sex), he's ready for a new challenge. Of course he can't let you know he only wants sex because he knows you're smart enough not to date a guy like that, so he presents himself as a *Good Guy*. He says all the right things, leads you to believe he cares, wins your heart and moves on after he's gotten what he wants.

> "... my number one goal was to have sex and get it as quick as possible without having to put in work. Sometimes it would take me a day, sometimes it would take me two weeks; two weeks was the most amount of time I would spend talking to the girl before I moved on if she didn't have sex."
>
> ~HIGH SCHOOL GUY

Type 2: The *Good Guy*—He truly cares about you, but may still want sex.

This guy genuinely cares about you and has no intention of ever hurting you in any way. He's the kind of guy most mothers would want their daughters to date—kind, trustworthy, loyal, respectful and charming. He doesn't pressure you for sex. As a matter of fact, he allows you to decide when you're ready. He tells you he's willing to wait as long as you need and even tells you he's okay with not having sex if that's what you want. Unfortunately, the media may have conditioned him to equate sex with love just as much as it may have conditioned you. So he may believe the only way to express his love for you is through sex. He has never learned the true meaning of love and hasn't considered the risk sex involves for either of you.

> "Before I heard your lecture, I thought sex was the only way to show your girl 'love,' but protecting the girl to show how much you love her is what I learned from you.

Now I know that if I really want to protect her, I will do what is best for her and stop having sex with her."

~ HIGH SCHOOL GUY

Type 3: The *Best Guy*—He loves you so much that he will do what is best for you.

This guy knows the difference between love and lust. He knows love gives and lust takes. He also knows love is selfless. He's willing to do what is best for you, even if it means sacrificing the pleasure he would get from sex. He's the type of guy who respects and treats you the same as he would want someone to respect and treat his little sister or future daughter. He's the guy who has dreams and goals and doesn't want to take part in any activity that would cause him to risk not reaching them. He also wants to protect your dreams and goals just as much as he protects his own. He would refuse to have sex with you even if you tried because he wants to protect you even when you won't protect yourself.

"I'm a month from being 17, and I'm still a virgin. I have chosen to be a virgin till marriage because I respect women too much to harm them in any way. I have been in one serious relationship in which my ex told me 'any time you want it just ask.' I had to tell her no, and I did not get into this relationship for sex. I hope this letter gets out to the girls you speak to because I want them to know that all guys aren't bad."

~ HIGH SCHOOL GUY

How can you tell the difference?

I wish there was a simple formula to tell right away which type of guy your boyfriend is. It's just not that easy. Most girls want to believe their boyfriend is the *Good Guy*, because—let's face it—who would be dumb enough to knowingly date the *Player*? And unfortunately, many girls don't believe *Best Guys* exist.

> *The enemy of best is not bad. The enemy of best is good.*

As you read the book and learn the secrets, it's important for you to understand that all three types do exist. Most people would warn you to watch out for the *Players*—and you do need to avoid those guys—but I think the *Good Guys* are the ones who have the best chance of getting you to have sex. After all, they don't have bad intentions. They truly care about you, and they may think sex is the best way to show it. In that case, if he really is a *Good Guy*, and you explain to him why sex is in neither of your best interests, then he should be completely on board.

Most importantly, by the end of this book, I want to give you hope there are not just *Players* and *Good Guys* out there, but *Best Guys* as well.

Why settle for a *Good Guy* when you could have a *Best Guy*? Now, let's get started sharing secrets . . .

WHAT KIND OF GUY DO YOU HAVE?

No need to wonder with this must-have cheat sheet that breaks down the three types of guys and how the 7 secrets apply to each one.

Download this cheat sheet NOW by going to:

www.7secretsofguys.com/cheatsheet

SECRET 1

Sex Doesn't Equal Love.

> "I had sex when I was in the seventh grade because I thought I was fat and ugly and nobody would ever want me. I did feel loved at some points, but you showed me just because someone has sex with you doesn't mean they love you."
>
>  HIGH SCHOOL GIRL

PLAYER	GOOD GUY	BEST GUY
Will tell you he loves you just to get sex, but he doesn't mean it.	May really care for you and still have sex with you because he has been misguided about sex and love just as much as you may have been.	He knows the best way to show you he loves you is to do what is best for you. He puts your best interest before his sex interest.

Identifying this first secret is what made me want to write this book. When I went into the classroom to talk about sex, the difference between girls' and guys' expectations couldn't have been more extreme. I asked girls what they wanted or expected

1

secret one

> It's unrealistic for a teenage girl to expect a short-term physical act to meet long-term emotional needs.

to get out of having sex. They gave answers like: love, commitment, closeness, intimacy, attention, affection and respect from their boyfriends. When guys answered the same question, they said: pleasure, respect from peers or bragging rights. As you can see, the guys made no mention of love. It's not that deep for them. Guys don't have to love you to have sex with you. And most guys aren't looking for love from you as a result of sex.

"My ex-girlfriend and I lost our virginities to each other freshman year. I feel she had sex to feel loved and special, as she isn't close with her dad. I just had sex because I wanted the pleasure."

~ HIGH SCHOOL GUY

Girls argue that guys expect too little from sex, while guys often tell me girls expect too much.

"When the girls said what they expect from sex, it was kind of eye opening. I don't understand why they would expect those things from a physical act."

~ HIGH SCHOOL GUY

Based on the girls' answers, I agree with the guys. It's unrealistic for a teenage girl to expect a short-term physical act to meet long-term emotional needs. Guys are much more likely to have their expectations met. But I also agree with the girls that guys expect too little. Sex should be more than just a means of getting pleasure.

Both sets of flawed expectations are based on misleading messages from the media and popular culture. Our culture has trivialized sex and love so much that many teens don't know what to expect. Because I wrote this book for teen girls, this chapter will focus on their unrealistic expectations instead of why the guys' expectations are too low. You'll also learn why girls are usually disappointed whenever they use sex to get love.

> "I agree that girls and guys want sex for different reasons. I had a bad experience in which I dated a guy for seven months, and I felt like I was in love; but after we had sex a few times, he broke up with me and told me it was practice for college."
>
> — HIGH SCHOOL GIRL

How is love portrayed in our culture?

The media often portrays love as an unrealistic, idealized whirlwind romance like those shown to little girls in movies. Many teenage girls have bought into that version of love, dreaming about the day their Prince Charming will rescue them and carry them away on a white horse to live happily ever after. Too often these girls are so eager for the fantasy they're ready to accept the first guy who shows interest as their Prince Charming—even if he doesn't have a horse or the best intentions.

Those girls who base their definition of love on what the media portrays, will read romance novels, watch movies and television shows or listen to love songs, and walk away believing sex is the natural way to show a guy they love him. The media is the last place you should look to define love. The movies don't normally last long enough for you to see the regrets of the people who gave their bodies away not realizing that pieces of their heart were being lost in the process.

What is love?

Today, if you're interested in knowing more about a topic, you can search online for it or talk to someone who may know something about the subject. If you do either on the topic of love, you'll most likely walk away more confused than you were before you started. Most of the information seems to boil down to two ways to describe love:

1. hormonal attraction, which is sometimes called "having chemistry," and
2. authentic love, which involves selflessness, commitment and wanting what's best for the other.

Many teens put too much focus on chemistry when choosing their partners and too little focus on authentic love. When it comes to having a healthy love relationship, the goal should be to have both. Too often, girls settle for the chemistry without demanding selfless love.

> "After listening to you in class, my boyfriend and I talked about love. I told him even though we have chemistry, we also need the selflessness. When we talked about sex, I told him I'm waiting until marriage. He got mad, which made me realize we should take a break."
>
> — HIGH SCHOOL GIRL

sex doesn't equal love

How can we be so confused about a topic that's so important and so longed for?

When talking with students, I hear two extreme reactions when I ask them to define love:

The negative and jaded . . .

- "Love is overrated."
- "The word *love* is thrown around so much that it has lost its meaning and value."
- "We're too young to know what love is."
- "I don't believe in love."

Or the superficial and naïve . . .

- "You just know it when you feel it."
- "It's hard to describe."
- "It's when you get that funny feeling in your stomach."
- "It's when you can't stop thinking about the person."

When I hear these types of comments, I realize these students don't know what love is. Often, they've confused love with infatuation. Infatuation is an intense but typically short-lived passion or admiration for someone. It's a natural part of a romantic relationship, but infatuation won't sustain a relationship for the long haul. It's the appetizer, not the meal. It's the preview of what's to come, not the movie itself.

> . . . but infatuation won't sustain a relationship for the long haul.

Authentic love is a decision that happens over time to commit oneself to another. It's also unconditional. You don't have to give anything like sex to get it or keep it.

secret one

"The most important thing I took from what you said is if someone loves you, they will want the best for you and won't make you do anything you don't want to do. This will now help me pick and choose the type of boys I want to give my time to."

❧ HIGH SCHOOL GIRL

Let's go over a few indicators to use when trying to decide whether you've found true love. Replace the word love below with your guy's name and see if he passes the test.

>   **LOVE** is honest and trustworthy.
>> **LOVE** is patient and doesn't rush me to do anything before I'm ready.
>>> **LOVE** isn't jealous.
>>>> **LOVE** cares as much about my welfare as he does his own.
>>>>> **LOVE** doesn't expect me to compromise my values.
>>>>>> **LOVE** is respectful.
>>>>>>> **LOVE** protects me.

So, how did your guy do? Hopefully, he measures up. If not, you should hold out for someone who does.

How is love shown?

"I used to think I loved my girlfriend, but we were considering sex. Now I know I truly love her because I

> wouldn't do anything that could possibly hurt her or damage her life, and that includes having sex."
>
> ~High School Guy

When I ask students whether sex is ever the best or wisest choice for teenagers, ninety-nine percent will say "No." Even those who are currently sexually active will admit having sex isn't the best way for them to reach their dreams, and therefore not the best choice for their lives.

When I ask students when is the best time for two people to have sex, I get many responses. They say when they're married, when they've graduated high school, when they've graduated college or when they can handle the consequences. But there's also usually someone (most often a girl) who will say, "As long as they are in love."

Guys often laugh at that response because they say guys don't have to love a girl to have sex with her. Of course, the girls who are sexually active with their boyfriends take offense to that.

After a lively discussion—which usually becomes a debate—about love and sex, an overwhelming majority of students will say even love isn't a valid reason for teenagers to have sex.

Students come to this conclusion for a few reasons:

1. Anyone could say they love you to get sex.
2. Love doesn't always last . . . especially not at our age.
3. Love doesn't pay bills or buy diapers, formula, etc.

But let's just assume love would be a good reason for teens to have sex. How do you know when you love someone? Most students will agree love is shown when you'll always do what's best for the other person and wouldn't do anything to harm

secret one

him or her. Of course, there are always mistakes made where someone may get hurt unintentionally even when in love. But, most students agree if one person does something knowing it could harm the other, that's not love.

So if both of those things are true—it's never the best choice for teens to have sex, *and* when you love someone you'll do what's best for them—then is it possible for teens to have sex and truly love each other? The vast majority of the class will say it's not. I agree!

There are still a few girls who may say it's possible for their boyfriends to love them and have sex with them. But, how is it possible for a guy to love a girl and ask her to do something that can harm her even more than it can harm him? The physical consequences of having sex will always be worse for girls than they are for guys. Guys can't get pregnant. Guys can't get cervical cancer and girls get sexually transmitted diseases (STDs) easier than guys do.

Some girls will still say having sex is okay, if the guy wasn't the one who initiated it. These girls will argue if the girl was the one who pushed for sex, then it's possible the guy does love her. These girls are still missing the point. Regardless of who initiates sex, she has to question his professed love if he takes part in an act that he knows could harm her even more than it harms him.

If he really loves you, you could come to him as naked as the day you were born and offer him sex on a silver platter. He would still say, "Baby, as hard as it is for me to not give in, I love you so much I'm going to do what's best for you, even when you won't do what's best for yourself." This is what the *Best Guy* does.

> *The physical consequences of having sex will always be worse for girls than they are for guys.*

If it's selfish, it's not love.

I made the above statement in one of my classes. A young man replied, "I can't love a girl enough to turn down sex if she's offering it to me, not as a teenager. I might be able to do it when I get older, but not now." He admitted real love would be able to turn down sex if it wasn't best for the other person. He just wasn't ready to put a girl's best interest before his sex interest. I appreciated that he was honest enough to admit he wasn't acting out of love.

It's difficult for young men like this one to turn down sex because for a teenage boy, sex is often about selfish pleasure. Selfish means lacking consideration for others, or concerned primarily with one's own personal profit or pleasure. When a guy isn't concerned with the risk to your health and future, and is more concerned with the pleasure he'll get from sex, he's being selfish.

Even the young man above realized his selfishness is—hopefully—temporary. Most teen boys will grow up to realize real love is selfless. It is more concerned with the needs and wishes of others than with one's own. But why risk your health and your future during your teen years on a guy who's not mature enough yet to be selfless?

> *When a guy isn't concerned with the risk to your health and future, and more concerned with the pleasure he'll get from sex, he's being selfish.*

CASE STUDY
Shelby and Josh

A former student named Shelby brought her boyfriend Josh to speak with me one day after class.

Shelby: Would you please tell my boyfriend what you told us in class about guys not being able to get tested for HPV (human papilloma virus)?

Me: She's right. There isn't a test for males to take to determine whether they have the type of HPV that could cause cervical cancer in females. The only way they will know they have the virus is if one of their partners tests positive for it.

Shelby: We've been having sex for three months. His ex-girlfriend and I are friends, and I know she has HPV because she told me. I want Josh to understand why I want to stop having sex because I don't want to put myself at risk of getting HPV any more than I already have.

Josh to Shelby: How do you know she didn't get the STD from someone she had sex with after we broke up? She might not have had it while we were dating.

Me to Josh: That's definitely a possibility, but it is just as possible she had it while you were dating.

Me to Shelby: How old are you?

Shelby: Seventeen.

> **Me to Josh:** Let me ask you a question. If you had a seventeen-year-old daughter or little sister, would you want her to be sexually active at that age?
>
> **Josh:** No.
>
> **Me:** Why?
>
> **Josh:** Because of the consequences.
>
> **Me:** Is that because you would love her too much to see her risk getting the consequences that may come with that decision?
>
> **Josh:** Exactly.
>
> **Me:** Why can't you love Shelby that much?
>
> **Josh:** I do love her. I've never pressured her to have sex.
>
> **Me:** If you really loved her, even if she pressured you to have sex, you wouldn't do it. You would do what's best for her even when she wouldn't do what's best for herself.

How is it possible for this young man to stand in front of his girlfriend and say he wouldn't want his own daughter or little sister to do the very thing he's asking her to do? *Real* love always does what's best for the other person. If this young man didn't think sex would be the best choice for his daughter or little sister, he should have respected his girlfriend enough not to let her make the same poor choice.

The next semester, I bumped into Shelby in the hallway and asked her how things were going with Josh. She told me they broke up. According to her, their breakup didn't have anything to do with him having HPV, things just didn't work out. I'm happy she was able to hear my message and hopefully it motivated her to stop having sex before becoming infected with HPV.

Why settle for sex when you're looking for real love?

> "I don't know real love. The first time I had sex I was just looking for love. I think that's the worst thing I could've done."
>
> — HIGH SCHOOL GIRL

> *Sex should never be the bait to get love or the only way to show love.*

Girls often tell me as the young lady above describes, they had sex as a way to feel loved or get a guy to love them. These young ladies have gotten things backward. Sex should never be the bait to get love or the only way to show love.

Sadly, a lot of girls still misunderstand the relationship between sex and the authentic love they really want. The following are just a few examples of when this happens:

1. A lot of young women have mistaken chemistry and infatuation for real love when butterflies and tingling feelings are only temporary.
2. Girls often think having sex is the key to unlock the real love they're seeking. They believe they'll get love from sex, which will fill the void they have inside. This expectation

falsely assumes sex has more power and influence than it does.

3. Some young women believe sex is required when you love someone, but it isn't. As we've already covered, authentic love doesn't need anything to keep it. It's unconditional.

"My girlfriend pressured me into sex my first time. In a way, it wasn't worth the risk, especially since I didn't love her."

～HIGH SCHOOL GUY

The above letter highlights two truths every girl must understand:

First, just because he's your boyfriend doesn't mean he loves you. When a girl attempts to justify her choice to have sex, she will say things like, "It's not like I'm having sex with a random guy. It's someone I'm in love with. We're in a relationship." This justification suggests being in a relationship is one and the same as being in love. Unfortunately, guys don't always see it the same way. As the above letter indicates, a guy can have a girlfriend without being in love with her.

> *…guys don't have to love you to have sex with you.*

Second, as mentioned earlier, guys don't have to love you to have sex with you. As a matter of fact, it's often easier for a guy to have sex with a girl without having feelings for her than it is for a girl to do the same. Many guys have even asked me why girls have to get so emotionally attached after having sex. It breaks my heart to speak to a girl who's devastated after realizing the sex meant much more to her than it did to her partner.

"Everything you talked about was basically my story. I learned love is not an excuse to have sex. I met a boy who showed me what love is when I thought love didn't exist. He made me feel like the prettiest girl in the world. He did a lot for me, and I wanted to give him something special, so I gave him my virginity. He never asked me to have sex with him; I just wanted him to be my first. Now that I have given him my virginity, I feel like he's using me for sex. After I heard you speak, I called him and asked him why does he have sex with me. He couldn't give me an answer. I told him why I have sex with him and he was shocked. He doesn't feel the same way, so now I'm hurt. I really thought he felt the same way. I made a mistake, but I will do better next time."

~HIGH SCHOOL GIRL

Love is almost never forever in high school.

A recent high school graduate talked to me one day about an issue he was having. He had been trying to end the relationship with his long-term girlfriend. She was having a hard time accepting the fact that he no longer wanted to be in a relationship with her. During our conversation, the subject of love came up, and the young man told me he could only love one thing at a time and currently he loved football.

I thought his statement was interesting, especially since he had admitted to being sexually active with his girlfriend. I asked him if he loved his girlfriend, and he reiterated that he *loved* football, which was his only focus at the moment. I asked him if he had ever told his girlfriend he loved her. He admitted he had, in fact, said those words.

I asked him why he would say it if he didn't mean it. He said, "She sort of forced me into telling her I loved her because she said it first. I just didn't want to hurt her feelings." If he really didn't want to hurt her feelings, he would have told her he didn't love her before they had sex. What he likely meant is he didn't want to say anything that might keep him from getting what he wanted.

He went on to make an even more critical point. He insisted that even if he did mean it when he told her he loved her, it wouldn't mean they'd be together forever like she expected. I asked him how he could not feel any guilt about having sex with her, especially since he knew she had stronger feelings for him than he had for her. He thought it was unfair to blame guys for leading girls on. He asked me, "Why should guys take all the blame? Shouldn't girls take some responsibility for reading too much into what love means for teen guys?" As much as I hate to admit it, he does have a point.

> *When you treat your dating relationship like it's a marriage, a breakup will feel like a divorce.*

This young man's girlfriend may be one of the girls who thinks it's acceptable for teens to have sex as long as they're in love. So when her boyfriend tells her he loves her, she believes him and sees it as a green light for sex. After all, they *are* in love—or so she thinks. Unfortunately, she doesn't realize she's the only one who's in love. He only said it to avoid hurting her feelings.

This is a common scenario and primarily the reason why girls are usually more devastated when the relationship ends than guys. They're looking for love and think sex is the way to get it, but come up empty in the end. When you treat your dating relationship like it's a marriage, a breakup will feel like a divorce.

The situation with the above couple also brings out an important point I've noticed for years. Girls often look for their validation through relationships. Guys tend to find their validation through accomplishments, as illustrated by the following letter from a young man:

> "I'm a sophomore and I play football, basketball and baseball. My girlfriend wants to have sex. But I'd rather wait until we're married. She's important, but I'm more focused on sports and college."
>
> ~High School Guy

Chase your dreams, not relationships.

A mother of two teens once shared with me how differently her son and daughter prepared for the first day of school. Her daughter and her daughter's friends spent at least two weeks agonizing over the outfits they would wear and how they would wear their hair. They treated the first day of school like it was a major production. Their entire focus was on how they would look, so they could feel pretty and get guys to notice them.

Her son didn't put any thought or attention into his attire or appearance on the first day of school. He threw on a pair of shorts and a t-shirt and headed out the door. Her son isn't unlike most boys who spend little time worried about how they look. It's not that they don't seek validation. Boys are typically brought up to seek validation through accomplishments like sports rather than through their appearance or the attention of others.

I read a quote once that so eloquently describes what I have seen for years.

> "Somewhere along the line we messed up. We told girls that it's okay to chase guys instead of their dreams. We told her that no matter how smart, beautiful or talented she was, her intelligence, beauty and talent could only be validated by a relationship. Somewhere we went wrong. And the world has suffered ever since."
>
> — MELISSA LEWIS, Blogger

Who should be your first love?

> "I've always had low self-esteem, and I felt if I had sexual intercourse with the guys I 'talked to,' then maybe I'd feel different about myself, but the feeling never changed... I spent most of my life trying to find a boy that can love me more than I can ever love myself."
>
> — HIGH SCHOOL GIRL

There's nothing wrong with anyone wanting to feel loved. It's a natural desire. However, there is a problem with girls seeking that love from guys through sex.

Though many girls don't realize it, they need to love themselves first. Not in a conceited way. Girls should genuinely value themselves and know their lives and bodies matter and deserve to be protected. The great news for young women is this validation and acceptance is something they must develop within. It's not something others can give or take away. Young women who never learn this unfortunately become adult women who look for that same validation from others.

> "You taught me what it means to value myself as a young woman. You changed my whole outlook on sex and taught me that I shouldn't have sex just to show somebody I love him. I need to love and value myself first and find someone who will respect me and only wants what's best for me."
>
> —High School Girl

Girls should genuinely value themselves and know their lives and bodies matter and deserve to be protected.

Relationships are not a measure of your worth.

A fourteen-year-old young lady approached me after class one day. She wanted advice about how to tell her boyfriend she wanted to stop having sex. When I gave her some suggestions, she said, "But what if he breaks up with me when I tell him?" I told her, "If he leaves you just because you won't have sex, that would mean he doesn't love you or deserve you." She said, "But then I'll be all alone," as if being without a relationship was the worst thing that could ever happen to her.

The young lady shared other things that were happening in this relationship. After listening to her, I told her it didn't sound like she loved herself. Shocked, she confidently declared, "I *do* love myself." I responded, "I don't mean you don't love the way you look. I'm talking about loving yourself enough to not take part in any behavior that could prevent you from being the best you can be."

Why do so few girls truly value and love themselves? There are probably as many answers to that question as there are days of the month, and we talk about several of them in later chapters. A few reasons include:

1. believing they're not valuable because their fathers did not value them enough to be actively involved in their lives;
2. comparing themselves to unrealistic images portrayed in the media; and
3. experiencing rape or molestation in the past (or other traumatic events), and not feeling like their lives matter anymore because they are "damaged goods."

If any of these apply to you, take time for self-exploration so you can discover what makes you unique and valuable and totally deserving of love. If you don't know where to start, some suggestions include:

1. Find your passion: Identify what you love to do and make sure you take part in those activities regularly.
2. Drop unrealistic expectations: Stop comparing yourself to the false images of beauty that the media portrays.
3. Keep a journal: Every day, write down three things you like about yourself that aren't based on how you look (i.e., sense of humor, kindness, strength, etc.) and read what you've written whenever you feel insecure.

4. Volunteer: Serve others because it will give you a sense of purpose and you'll feel better about yourself.
5. Surround yourself with positivity: Find inspirational quotes that speak to you and hang them up in your locker or on your mirror as a daily reminder to stay positive.

Once you value yourself, you won't fall for any of those counterfeit versions of love.

Now that you know . . .

Now that you've seen plenty of misconceptions about love, I hope you'll be able to determine what's real and what's not. Don't fall for the fictitious version of love or simple physical chemistry. Demand more. Fairytale romances are great to read about or watch at the movies, but they're not a realistic depiction of the true love you seek. Sure, chemistry is great to have, but it's not enough to sustain a healthy, whole relationship. You are worthy of a love that honors your values, your dreams and your wellbeing, so don't settle for anything less.

Remember, real love looks out for the best interests of the other person and doesn't cost anything. If you have to risk your own health and future to get it, it's not real love. Most importantly, if you love yourself first, you won't settle for anything less from others.

> "Your words helped me to realize how important I was to my boyfriend and myself. I thought maybe my boyfriend and I should have sex—after all we both love each other and our hormones were running rampant. It wasn't until after I expressed my thoughts

sex doesn't equal love

to my boyfriend and listened to your definition of love did I realize my idea of love was slightly skewed and that my boyfriend truly loves me. My boyfriend said that he would never pressure me to have sex with him and he himself wasn't ready for such a milestone. 'Our futures are big and bright,' he said, 'especially yours. And I would not be a man that loves you if I allow you to participate in something that has the potential to wreck your bright and beautiful future.'"

— HIGH SCHOOL GIRL

FREE VIDEO BONUS

Hear what a guy has to say about the 7 secrets. Watch the videos NOW by going to:

www.7secretsofguys.com/videos

SECRET 2

They'll tell you what you want to hear.

"Before you spoke to my class, I didn't believe I could wait for sex. All my friends had been doing it, and it tempted me to try. I was just waiting for the 'right' guy to come along and tell me what I wanted to hear."

— HIGH SCHOOL GIRL

PLAYER	GOOD GUY	BEST GUY
Lies just to get sex.	Sometimes lies to avoid hurting your feelings.	Doesn't lie.

"I became sexually active at a very young age. I knew all the tricks: find a girl, say what she wanted to hear, have sex that night."

— HIGH SCHOOL GUY

A lot of girls think they're too smart to fall for the same old tricks, but not all guys are as transparent as the one quoted above. Most guys know how to navigate relationships with girls the same way they handle any other relationship: by telling people what they want to hear. The same way you may have told your parents a lie because you knew it's what they wanted to hear, boys may say whatever it is they think will work best on you.

Why do guys tell you what you want to hear?

There are three reasons guys will tell you what you want to hear, even if they know it's not the truth: to get what they want, to avoid hurting your feelings and because you won't always accept the truth.

1 They want sex.

> "Two years ago, a week after my sixteenth birthday, I gave up my virginity to a guy I knew at church. That's all our relationship ever was—just sex. He wasn't my boyfriend at the time. He was just a friend who knew about my depression problems and my low self-esteem. He said all the right words that I wanted to hear just so he could get into my pants. It worked. I cried later that week when I found out he was lying about everything he told me. He told me straight up that he couldn't take me seriously as a girlfriend and that all I was good for was sex."
>
> — HIGH SCHOOL GIRL

It's quite common for a girl to have sex with a guy to feel loved and for a guy to act like he loves a girl to get sex. The *Player* already knows a girl will give the physical to get the emotional. So if he has to fake the emotional by telling her what she wants to hear to get sex, he will.

Unfortunately, this scenario rarely turns out well for young ladies. They always get the short end of the stick because when the relationship ends, the guys got what they wanted and the girls often didn't.

The average teen girl is looking for long-term intimacy and closeness in a relationship. She most often has sex to feel that emotional connection. She thinks, *If I need to have sex to feel an emotional connection, I will.*

I encountered one frustrated young lady who yelled at the guys in class, "Why can't y'all just tell us the truth? If all you want is sex, you should just say that up front instead of making us think you really love us. Because we get our hopes up and our emotions involved, and then we're devastated when y'all leave. I don't understand why guys just can't be honest."

One of the guys responded, "Because that's the best part of the game."

Spoken like a true player.

I wanted to offer a different explanation to help the young lady understand. So I asked her, "Would you have sex with a guy who told you up front he didn't love you, but wanted to have sex with you?" She said, "No." I responded, "And that's why they aren't honest with you upfront. Because they know if they are, you won't have sex with them."

> It's quite common for a girl to have sex with a guy to feel loved and for a guy to act like he loves a girl to get sex.

2 They don't want to hurt your feelings.

> *"Girls say they want the truth from us, but they really don't. I dated a girl once who told me she loved me. I thought she was crazy because I didn't even know her favorite color yet. When I told her I didn't feel the same way, she was devastated and got really angry. Said I was mean and heartless. I wish I had said it back to her just to keep the peace."*
>
> —HIGH SCHOOL GUY

The *Good Guy* is most often the one guilty of this lie. He isn't motivated by sex. He's just trying to avoid hurting your feelings. I asked one such boy if he'd ever been in love, and this was his response:

Him: Have I ever said it or have I ever felt it?

Me: If the answer isn't the same for both questions, let's start with have you ever said it?

Him: Yes.

Me: Well, have you ever felt it?

Him: No.

Me: If you didn't feel it, why did you say it?

Him: Because she said it first. What was I supposed to say? It was awkward.

Me [Jokingly]: You say, "Me too." Get it, I love me too.

In this young man's mind, he lied to her so he wouldn't look like a jerk. In fact, I'm sure he thought lying was the nice thing to do. The problem arises when young ladies place too much stock in those three words. Many feel obligated to have sex to prove to guys they love them too. Or even worse, they reciprocate with sex as if to say, "Thank you for loving me."

So imagine the girl who's dating the guy above who has said he loves her but doesn't mean it. Unlike the guys who lie just to get what they want, this young man may not have started out trying to deceive his girlfriend to get sex. Remember, he's the *Good Guy*. His desire to avoid hurting her just happens to work in his favor because she also believes love makes sex in a relationship acceptable. Unfortunately, she's the only one who is "in love." He doesn't think he's using her because he does actually care for her—he just doesn't love her.

3 Girls won't accept the truth.

> *"My ex-girlfriend and I were having sex, and we ended up breaking up after a few months. I was not attached, however, she became obsessive and texted me and called a lot after the breakup. I ended up having to block her on all social media sites. I now realize it was wrong to use her for my own sexual selfishness. I now vow to abstain from sexual intercourse until I meet the woman I wish to spend the rest of my life with."*
>
> — High School Guy

Even when this young man wanted to end the relationship, the young lady thought she could change his mind. But if he *had* continued dating her as a result of her begging, the relationship would have been built on a lie. Young ladies, please don't be so afraid of being alone that you beg the guy to stay in a relationship he's already told you he doesn't want to be in.

Even if he stays, his heart isn't in the relationship. He's more than likely trying to figure out a different exit strategy that will bring less drama. The following conversation I had with a young man is a prime example.

> **CASE STUDY**
> *Sean and Amber*
>
> **Sean:** I want to tell you about my situation to show you it's not always the guys' fault that girls get hurt. Girls get themselves into bad situations just 'cause they don't want to accept the truth.
>
> **Me:** Even though I never said it was always the guys' fault, I'm all ears. Tell me how girls get themselves in bad situations.
>
> **Sean:** Well, my girlfriend, Amber, and I have been dating for two years. The first year, everything was good, and I even thought I could have married her someday. But, after that first year, things started to change. I realized I couldn't trust Amber like I thought I could, and I just didn't see a future with her after all. Over the past couple months, I've tried to break up with her several times, and she won't let me do it.
>
> **Me:** What do you mean she won't let you break up with her?
>
> **Sean:** Every time I tell her we need to end the relationship, she starts crying and begging me to stay.

One time she started saying she didn't want to live without me, and I got worried she might be suicidal. I felt so sorry for her I decided not to end it.

Me: If I were a teenage girl, I wouldn't want someone staying with me just because he felt sorry for me.

Sean: Ms. Jackie, you don't know these girls today. They're crazy. But, it's cool. I figured out how to handle it. I graduate in six months, and I'm planning to join the military, so I'll just stick it out until then. I figure once I leave, things will just fizzle out while I'm away and that way I won't have to deal with all the drama of the breakup.

Me: Let me ask you a personal question, and you don't have to answer it. Are the two of you sexually active?

Sean: Yes. We've been having sex for about a year and a half.

Me: During the next six months when you're "sticking it out," do you plan to continue having sex with her?

Sean: Of course. Sex is the only thing that will make it bearable.

Me: You do know a pregnancy could happen during the next six months, don't you? Can you imagine how much more difficult it will be to end the relationship if Amber gets pregnant? If you think she's crazy now, how much more crazy will she act if she has a child with you and you try to leave her?

Sean: Oh, I use a condom *every* time. I'm not trying to have a kid with her.

secret two

> **Me:** Do you know how many stories I hear about condoms breaking? The only way to eliminate the possibility of her getting pregnant is not to have sex.
>
> **Sean:** Man, I thought I had the situation all worked out, but you're right. If she gets pregnant, it will be ten times worse. Now I have to decide which is worse: dealing with the drama of a nasty breakup now or staying with her for six months without sex. Maybe you can explain to her why she should let me go.
>
> **Me:** Nope, this is something you have to do.

I bet Amber didn't have a clue she was having sex with someone who was counting down the days until he could be out of the relationship. Amber thought she was able to change Sean's mind and make him see the error of his ways while he was just trying to tell her the truth. In her mind, they were together because he still loved her. In his mind, he had already left. His body was just hanging around for the benefits.

Whose fault is it that she didn't know? We can say Sean is terrible and shouldn't use Amber for sex, but what responsibility must Amber take in this situation? When Sean tried to end the relationship, she refused to believe or accept he no longer wanted to be with her.

No, there is never a good reason to lie in a relationship. That said, young ladies, there are times when girls must take some responsibility for a guy feeling a lie is his only choice. Ask yourself this, "Do I always want to hear the truth, even if it means I won't get what I want, which is a relationship?" A lot of girls might answer no to this question. Many would choose to reject the truth rather than face the fact that the guy doesn't feel the same way about them as they feel about him.

I have seen too many young ladies (and adult women) think they can change guys' minds or they can help them make up their minds. Believe me, a guy knows what and whom he wants, and no amount of begging will convince him otherwise.

Young women have to stop basing their value on whether they are in a relationship or having sex. Instead of being afraid to be alone or thinking that having a boyfriend validates you, spend your teen years figuring out who you are, what you like/dislike and how you can make a difference in the world.

> *Young women have to stop basing their value on whether they are in a relationship or having sex.*

What's a common way guys lie to get sex?

A lot of players will use reverse psychology to get what they want. With this method, guys can get you to do what they want you to do by pretending they want the opposite.

For example, I once had a "super senior"—someone who is repeating the twelfth grade—in one of my classes. He was also a self-proclaimed sex expert. Over my two days at his school, this young man felt a need to comment on everything I said. Maybe if he'd known as much about his education as he pretended to know about sex, he wouldn't be repeating a grade—just saying.

At one point, this young man decided to teach the younger students in class about the best way to get girls to have sex with them. To my surprise, he did share information that was worthwhile, which is why I'm sharing it here with you.

He said, "The best way to get a girl to have sex with you is to act like you don't want it because that way you earn her trust. As a matter of fact, she goes back to her friends bragging to them about the fact that she has a *Good Guy* because you're not pressuring her to have sex. Before long, she'll offer sex to you. For some reason, girls feel better about having sex if you don't pressure them into it and they think it was their decision."

Unfortunately, many girls confirm the effectiveness of what this guy said. I've heard plenty of girls say, "But he didn't pressure me. It was my decision. So it's not like he's using me." They even feel sorry for those other girls whose boyfriends didn't love them enough to wait until they were ready for sex. They don't realize they too are playing right into the guys' hands.

When this boy finished dropping his super senior wisdom on his younger classmates, several guys high fived him, laughed and confirmed they used the same strategy. One guy in the class even got mad at him for "ruining their game." Of course, *Players* don't want that secret to get out because if it does, their *Good Guy* disguise will be blown.

Isn't it amazing how easily they have figured out what it takes to get sex from girls? I see guys using reverse psychology on girls all the time.

> "When you said 'the guy gives you freedom to decide about sex so he can earn your trust' is 'game,' you were not lying. That's exactly how my situation happened. I was very vulnerable when we had sex . . . He played me, and I fell for his lies. Ever since that day I have been depressed and distant from all that are close to me. I don't trust anyone anymore. No girl should experience this pain."
>
> HIGH SCHOOL GIRL

A ninth-grade girl once bragged about her boyfriend because he had not pressured her into sex. She said, "My friends [all freshmen] and I date upperclassmen guys. My boyfriend is the only one who hasn't pressured me into having sex. He told me he was willing to wait until I was ready." She felt like her boyfriend cared more for her than her friends' boyfriends cared for them because he allowed her to decide when sex would happen. I was quick to point out to her the fact that he allowed her to decide when sex would happen just meant he was more patient than her friends' boyfriends. It didn't mean he loved her any more. He just had a different strategy. If he loved her, he wouldn't have sex with her even if that were what she wanted.

A guy at another school told me when guys tell girls they don't want to have sex, it just makes girls more attracted to them. This guy wasn't using this to his advantage and trying to run game. He was frustrated by the fact that guys can't seem to win. Even if they don't want to have sex or are having sex and want to stop, it's difficult because girls then put even greater pressure on them to have sex.

> "There's this girl who likes me a lot, and she wants to have sex. After you came and talked to us, I have completely stopped talking to her because she's crazy and will not leave me alone until I have sex with her."
>
> ~HIGH SCHOOL GUY

I'm not sure why this is the case. Is it because girls see refusal as a challenge, or because the refusal makes him more attractive because she now sees him as one of the *Good Guys*? Either way, it works against these girls in the long run.

secret two

What are the common lines guys use?

There are many lines guys use when trying to get a girl to have sex. We'll address six of those lines in this section:

1. I love you.
2. I won't tell.
3. I won't leave you.
4. I'm a virgin.
5. I'm clean.
6. I think you're different.

1 I love you.

> "I started having sex my first year of high school. Out of my whole four years I have had nine sexual partners. I lowered myself and gave into guys who told me those three words every girl wants to hear: 'I love you.'"
>
> — HIGH SCHOOL GIRL

{ **31%** [of guys] have lied about being in love when they knew they weren't or they weren't sure. }

Why are girls longing to hear those three words? I wish there were a simple answer, but there isn't. When a girl doesn't feel loved or love herself, hearing a guy say he loves her takes on more importance than it should because she needs validation. She is then vulnerable to guys taking advantage of her and, unfortunately, it may not even bother her.

I heard a speaker share a story about a young lady he'd counseled in the past. This young lady was sexually active but said she knew the guys didn't love her and were just using her for sex. The speaker asked her why she would continue to have sex with these guys when she knew they were only telling her they loved her to get sex from her. Her response saddened me. "I'd rather hear 'I love you' fake than never hear it at all." This response sounds extreme, but the behavior isn't as uncommon as you may think. There are many girls who feel the same way. They may not say those words, but the sentiment and their actions are the same nonetheless.

> "L.O.V.E. stands for **L**egs **O**pen **V**ery **E**asily."

An eighth-grade guy asked me one day if I knew what **L.O.V.E.** stood for. His definition surprised me. He said, "L.O.V.E. stands for **L**egs **O**pen **V**ery **E**asily." As crazy as this sounds, the sad reality is there's a lot of truth to what he said. Far too many girls are willing to do a lot in the name of "L.O.V.E."

2 I won't tell.

> "Before we had sex, I made him promise he wouldn't tell a soul. So I thought he wouldn't. But that next day at school, nobody except him and my best friend liked me. I was a hoe . . . to everyone—just because I had sex one time. I didn't understand at all how I was all those things when he did it too but everyone liked him still."
>
> — Middle School Girl

Far too many times, young ladies have cried in my arms because they got a bad reputation when the word got out

secret two

they'd had sex. In every situation, these girls trusted the guys too soon. They believed the guys when they said they wouldn't tell. After all, they "promised" they wouldn't. In our society, a guy can have as much sex as he wants without a negative reputation, while a girl can have sex one time and get labeled. I hate this unfair double standard, but this point isn't about the double standard. This is about girls trusting guys who are untrustworthy.

The following story from one of my classes is a prime example of a girl trusting a guy who wasn't trustworthy.

A senior football player appeared to be in real agony at different points on both days of the class discussion. If he could've put his fingers in his ears to block out the truth he was hearing, he would have done so.

I saw pain on his face every time I talked about guys treating young ladies with respect, not doing anything with a girl they wouldn't want someone to do with their daughters or little sisters and being protectors and not predators. I figured he was currently sexually active (and he may have been).

On the second day, he asked if he could speak with me after class. He and three of his teammates spent their lunch period talking with me. First, he said, "Ms. Jackie, prom is Friday night, and I want you to know you messed up my prom plans. After hearing you the first day, I realized I couldn't have intercourse. But I was still planning on oral sex. Then today you had to show us the video of the dentist revealing that oral sex causes oral cancer. So now I'm even afraid to do that. You're taking everything from us."

I responded, "I'm not taking anything from you because I'm not the sex police. I'm just giving you information that could prevent you from experiencing some consequences you don't want."

I asked him about the girl he was taking to prom and found out she wasn't even his girlfriend.

His friend chimed in, "But she's been trying to get with him since middle school," as if that made the casual sex acceptable.

To justify his intention to have sex with a girl he wasn't in a relationship with, he told me sex on prom night was her idea.

He even showed me her text messages to prove it. They were XXX rated to say the least. She went into graphic detail about what she wanted him to do and how she wanted him to do it. She also told him what she would gladly do to him. My mouth was open in shock the entire time I read the text messages.

> *Any guy who's willing to have sex with a girl he's not even dating won't have a problem telling his friends about it.*

In one of the text messages, she told him she didn't want him to tell anyone about them having sex because it was very personal to her. How about that! Not only did he tell me, but his three friends also knew about the plan to have sex. It was clear he had also allowed them to read all her graphic text messages.

I pointed out he'd violated her trust by sharing her conversation with his friends. He responded, "These are my homeboys. I don't keep anything from them."

It amazes me that young ladies are naïve enough to believe guys keep things like this a secret. Any guy who's willing to have sex with a girl he's not even dating won't have a problem telling his friends about it.

The young man was looking over my shoulder as I read the messages. When I got to his response to her, he took the phone before I could read his texts and said I had read enough. I said,

"So you don't want me to read what you texted because you want to protect your image, but you don't care about hers." He just laughed.

Though I scolded this young man for his actions, I couldn't help but feel a deep sadness for the girl. If she didn't want anyone to know they had sex, I can only imagine she didn't want anyone to see the graphic text messages either. It breaks my heart to see this girl, and so many others, put so much trust in guys who don't have their best interest at heart.

If a guy tells you he won't tell anyone if the two of you have sex, assume the opposite is true. And while his sexual prowess is high-fived, you may be "slut shamed." I'm sure that's not what any girl signs up for when she agrees to sex, but this is the reality. What's more, it's not just sex they vow to keep a secret. Just as the young man, mentioned above, shared the young lady's private text messages with his friends even after she requested her privacy, there are guys who have no problem sharing inappropriate pictures of girls with their friends as well.

> "Two years ago I was talking to a guy when he asked me for a picture. I said no, but he begged me and said he loved me and I could trust him, so I did. He showed it to his friends and I was so upset. Now, it's hard to trust guys."
>
> —High School Girl

3 I won't leave you.

> "He told me he would never leave me, and he would always be there no matter what. During this time, we had sexual intercourse eight times. After a while I felt as if I couldn't live without him. By the time school started I

realized he wasn't who he portrayed himself to be. By the first month of school, he and I had completely stopped talking, and he started to go out with my friend."

                                                                   HIGH SCHOOL GIRL

    I'll never forget the young lady I spoke with years ago who tried her best to convince me it wasn't a bad idea for her to have sex with her boyfriend. I brought it to her attention if she got pregnant a baby would likely change her life much more than her boyfriend's. She informed me she and her boyfriend had already had the discussion about how they would handle a pregnancy should they experience one. He "promised" her he would stay with her and help take care of the baby, and she believed him.

    I looked her in the eyes and asked if she expected him to tell her the truth and say, "Baby, if you get pregnant, I'm going to leave, just like most guys do when they get a teen girl pregnant." A lot of girls can be naïve when it comes to their boyfriends.

"I am one of those girls that fell for that type of guy that said all the right things and did all the wrong things. I got pregnant at fifteen. He said he'd stay and take care of our baby. He did not help me with anything, and I eventually stopped talking to him."

                                                                   HIGH SCHOOL GIRL

4 I'm a virgin.

". . . I lost my virginity to a guy I was 'in love with' . . . soon to find out it was just lust. He told me he was a

> virgin, and I found out later that he had slept with my best friend. So not only have I slept with him, but also my bestie and all her past partners. I learned a lot from this talk—that you can change and wait, even if you're not a virgin."
>
> — MIDDLE SCHOOL GIRL

High school guys have told me they will lie about being a virgin, as well as the number of previous sexual partners, to make girls feel safer. Wouldn't you feel safer if a guy told you he was a virgin or had only had one prior sexual partner, even though you were his tenth? Even if his number of sexual partners is low, girls don't think about how many partners his partners have had. Know this: When you have sex with someone, there's not just a co-mingling of bodies, but of histories as well.

5 I'm clean.

Even worse than lying about their sexual histories, guys will lie about STDs.

> "Before you came, I was ready to have sex with the guy I've been in love with for six months. After you came, we went to go get tested, and it turned out he had herpes. I was surprised because he had already known he had herpes for three years and was still going to have sex with me."
>
> — HIGH SCHOOL GIRL

they'll tell you what you want to hear

I'm happy to see that this young lady asked about STDs before having sex, and was wise enough to get tested. This isn't normally the case. A lot of girls avoid this topic because they think asking about STDs is awkward and implies they believe the other person is promiscuous. What you need to know is you don't have to have a lot of sexual partners to contract an STD. You can get an STD after only one sexual encounter, as was the case for the young lady mentioned in this email from a health teacher:

> "I have a student who is at a loss for words. She recently had sex for the first time and contracted herpes. She is a mess and is seeking guidance from me. I am not sure what to tell her. I'd appreciate any input you could provide."

Consequences like these are why it's imperative you have the STD discussion. And even then, know if you have the conversation, there's no guarantee you'll get the truth. Even if he shares that he got tested, how do you know if he's been tested for all twenty-five-plus diseases? Also, has he remained celibate since he was tested? Are you willing to risk your own health to find out the hard way? Additionally, there's no test for a guy to determine if he has the most common viral STD: Human Papilloma Virus (HPV)—even if you get the HPV vaccine, it doesn't cover every strain of the virus, and you may still become infected.

Why would a person lie about having STDs? Well, would you have sex with a guy who told you he had an STD? Probably not. Guys with STDs know that, so they're motivated to lie to get sex.

secret two

> *…STDs don't discriminate. They don't care what gender your partner is.*

But let's be clear, guys aren't the only ones lying. A lesbian young lady spoke to me after class one day and told me her ex-girlfriend had herpes. Yet the ex-girlfriend was continuing to have sex with girls and guys without telling them she had herpes. She had already infected at least one girl at their school with herpes. Who knows how many more were infected? Then consider them passing it to their other partners. You can see how important it is to know the status of the person you're with.

Speaking of girls having sex with girls, I need to mention that STDs don't discriminate. They don't care what gender your partner is. Many girls think they don't have to worry about negative consequences because they're having sex with another girl and can't get pregnant or contract an STD. But, same sex does not equal safe sex. The only thing same gender couples don't have to worry about is pregnancy. They're still at risk of STDs and emotional consequences.

6 I think you're different.

> *"Before you came, I had been talking to a boy that I had known for a long time. I knew that he had had sex with a lot of girls and flirted with girls. I was thinking of having sex with him because he made me feel special and different. I'm glad I didn't because now I know I was just another girl to him."*
>
> — HIGH SCHOOL GIRL

Thank goodness the young lady who wrote the above letter realized before having sex with this guy that to him, she would be no different than all the other girls he'd had sex with. Far too many girls aren't this fortunate.

I understand why guys who don't have a good track record in their relationships feel the need to convince any future girlfriend that things will be different with her. I'm just surprised by how many girls believe them. For example, if he cheated on the last girl he dated, he won't be faithful to you, and definitely not if you're the girl he cheated with. As my mother always said, "You'd better believe if he'll cheat with you, he'll cheat on you." In more extreme cases, if he didn't stay with the last girl he got pregnant, the chances of him staying with you if you get pregnant aren't high. Girls could save themselves a lot of heartache and disappointment if they would consider relationship history when deciding whether to date a guy.

> *"You'd better believe if he'll cheat with you, he'll cheat on you."*

Why do girls believe the lies?

First, I'll give you the most obvious reason I think girls believe the lies, then I'll talk about a deeper reason most teens don't even consider.

> *"You made me realize I let guys talk me into having sex when it is not what I want to do. I never wanted to be the girl guys pass in the hallway and whisper to their friends, "I hit that one," but I am . . . I convinced myself*

secret two

they cared and let myself believe the lies because I needed the attention."

— HIGH SCHOOL GIRL

> *Seeking guidance on big decisions from your friends or peers doesn't make sense because their brains aren't any more developed than yours.*

This young lady hit the nail on the head for the most obvious reason girls believe the lies. They want to be in a relationship so badly they will convince themselves the guys mean what they say. Their need for a relationship can often stem from a need to feel loved and cared for, which I spoke about in Chapter 1.

The second and deeper reason girls believe the lies has to do with a teen's brain development. The last part of the brain to develop is the part that associates consequences with decisions. It won't fully develop until you're in your early to mid-twenties. As a teenager, decisions are primarily made based on impulse and emotions.

Combine the emotions with the hormones, and it's easy to understand why teens may make some poor decisions when it comes to relationships. This is why a teenage girl can know about the risks of having sex but still choose to do it because of the intense emotions she feels for her boyfriend. This is also why she can get caught up in the heat of the moment with someone she may not even know and make an impulsive decision to have sex. No matter how smart she is, her emotions are still ruling her choices. She's not considering the potential consequences of her decisions.

Seeking guidance on big decisions from your friends or peers doesn't make sense because their brains aren't any more developed than yours. It's important to seek out and follow advice from adult figures when making big choices. Sex is definitely one of many major decisions that you should discuss with the adults in your life.

More specifically, you should seek advice from a mature adult. Notice I said mature adult because some adults older than twenty-five still behave as if their brains haven't fully developed either. Hint: If they're doing the same things you're doing, they are not mature.

The following analogy describes what it's like if/when you choose to make major decisions on your own without listening to the counsel of mature adults:

> You're swimming through shark-filled waters, which is what today's culture is like. There are "sharks" out there waiting to eat you alive—drugs, alcohol, sex, violence, etc. Your parents and/or other adults are overhead looking down. They know exactly where the sharks are, for a couple of reasons.
>
> First, they have either swam through those same shark-filled waters before and have gained experiences that can help you. Or secondly, based on the fact that their brains are fully developed, they're in a better position to see the possible consequences.
>
> Unfortunately, too many teens think adults are out of touch or just don't want adults in their business. As a result, these teens don't seek out adults' counsel or just ignore their advice. This behavior is like saying, "Let me swim with my own sharks."

For example, one of my mentees called me from college once to ask what I thought about her going to the beach with three of her friends. It sounded innocent enough at first. It got more interesting when she told me she would be sharing the hotel room with one of her female friends and two male friends. She was so focused on getting to the beach and saving money she overlooked and minimized the other obvious factors. Neither of the girls knew the guys very well. They were setting themselves up for potential consequences that included assault, theft, rape or worse. The good news is she trusted me enough to not get upset by my questions or refuse my advice. Ironically, all her friends she sought advice from encouraged her to go and enjoy the weekend. Ultimately, that beach adventure didn't take place.

You must have a mature figure you trust in your lives who can give you advice in situations like the one above, when you and your friends may not be setting yourselves up to make the best decisions.

Now that you know . . .

Keep in mind there is nothing inherently wrong with being emotional. The problem comes when you allow your emotions to control your decision-making. When you meet a guy who doesn't necessarily have your best interest at heart, he'll capitalize on your emotional decision-making by telling you exactly what you want to hear. This is why you have to be careful who you allow to enter your heart because your heart can't always be trusted. Your heart will cloud your judgment. It will prematurely see feelings that don't exist, and it will put up with lies to protect itself. When it comes to having a healthy relationship with a guy, it's always best to let your head take the lead and let your heart follow suit. Don't fall for what sounds good. Stand for what you know is right.

> "I lost my virginity to my ex-boyfriend last year because I believed he was going to be my forever. I shared everything with him. I trusted him with my life, and he ended up betraying me in every way imaginable. I realize now that I trusted him way too early in the relationship. I feel like if we hadn't had sex, he wouldn't have made a fool out of me because I would have been able to see through his lies. I'm definitely not having sex with the next guy I date because I don't want my emotions to get me in trouble again."
>
> — HIGH SCHOOL GIRL

SECRET 3

They won't respect you if you don't respect yourself.

"I was close to giving it up to a boy who wasn't even my boyfriend. You helped me realize I should value myself more. The talk you gave us made me realize if I can't respect myself why should a guy that I would have been intimate with respect me?"

— HIGH SCHOOL GIRL

PLAYER	GOOD GUY	BEST GUY
Disrespects you.	Does not intentionally disrespect you. May not see having sex with you as disrespecting you, but it is.	Will intentionally respect you, even if you don't respect you.

"Even though I would be upset if someone did with my future daughter what I am doing with the girls I date,

> I never felt bad about it because I didn't force them to have sex. If they don't value and respect themselves enough to say no to sex, why should I feel bad about having sex with them?"
>
> ~ HIGH SCHOOL GUY

Respect earns respect.

If you've never heard of the MTV show *Sex . . . with Mom and Dad*, rest assured it's not a show about having sex with parents. Instead, it's about discussing sex with parents in an educational and productive way.

Parents bring their teens on the show for an intervention due to their risky and potentially dangerous behavior. In one episode, a sixteen-year-old girl was sneaking out at night and sneaking guys in the house after the parents went to bed. She was having sex with guys she wasn't in a relationship with. She even talked to one of her boyfriends about wanting to have a baby while she was still a teenager. "Dr. Drew" Pinsky's intervention required the young lady to invite three of her previous boyfriends/sex partners over to her house for dinner with her parents. Awkward. During dinner, she had to ask the young men questions from cards provided by Dr. Drew.

One of the questions was, "What do you think I need to learn about relationships?" One young man answered: "I don't know about just relationships, but when you [are] talking to a dude, period . . . the respect you have for yourself, that's how the dude is gonna treat you. If [a girl] doesn't show that much respect for herself, then I'm not gonna give her that much respect." The guy knew sneaking in and out of the house to have casual sex with her was disrespectful to her and her parents, but

they won't respect you if you don't respect yourself

he did it because she let him. When she didn't respect herself and her parents' house, he didn't either.

That video clip has become one of my powerful teaching tools. It shows just how important it is for young women to respect themselves so guys will respect them. Ideally, all boys would respect young ladies regardless of how young ladies value themselves, but that's just not the case. It's so important for young ladies to be aware of how this young man—and most guys—think about respect.

What is self-respect?

> "I thought if I let boys touch me and twerk like everyone else then I would be respected. I also thought being a teenager means making mistakes like drinking and having sex. After your talk, I realize I will get respected for respecting myself."
>
> — Middle School Girl

self-re·spect
noun
pride and confidence in oneself; a feeling that one is behaving with honor and dignity.

Imagine how many bad decisions you could avoid if you only made decisions you could be proud of.

Imagine how many bad decisions you could avoid if you only made decisions you could be proud of. What if the following announcement came over the intercom every morning in your classroom?

"The following people had sex last night . . ."

If you're proud of that decision, you may even tell your friends to quiet down so they can hear them call your name. But if you wouldn't want anyone else to find out about it, that's a good sign you're not proud of the decision and it may not have been for the best. Self-respect and pride go hand in hand. It's difficult to have one without the other.

> *"Pride is a better motivator than fear."*
>
> ~ JOHN WOODEN, UCLA's legendary basketball coach

Most adults attempting to persuade you to abstain from sex focus on the physical consequences that may come from being sexually active. Although I think it's important for you to know about the physical consequences (and they are real), these aren't the only reasons to abstain from sex. Fear of consequences is certainly a deterrent, but it's always short lived. Your fear will go away in the heat of the moment, and you may find yourself making the decision you declared you wouldn't. Instead, I want you to make your decision to abstain from sex because of the pride you get from respecting yourself, like the young lady who wrote the letter below:

> *"A few months back a guy I really liked asked me if I was open to sex. I told him no only because I was scared to get pregnant, and I could not imagine my dad's face if I had to tell him I was pregnant. But after listening to your presentation, I no longer want to wait for sex because I'm scared. I want to wait because I have more*

value than to just give it away to some guy who 'says' he loves me."

🌹 HIGH SCHOOL GIRL

The decision to abstain from sex should be motivated by benefits, not consequences. And there is no greater motivation than feeling good about yourself and being proud of your choices.

> *The decision to abstain from sex should be motivated by benefits, not consequences.*

How can a guy tell whether you respect yourself?

Remember the three types of guys we've been discussing in each chapter? Well, they are all eager to see whether you respect yourself or not. What they will do if they realize you don't is different depending on which type of guy you're dealing with.

The guy we're most likely talking about in this section is the *Player*. Once he realizes you don't respect yourself, he's excited because he thinks he'll get sex in the end. Remember, most girls aren't aware they are dating this type until after he has gotten what he wants.

> "The morning I lost my virginity was the morning my boyfriend told me it was over. The entire morning, he kept trying and trying, but I said no, and after I had heard enough, I said yes. Everything after that was all downhill. I had plans and a life ahead of me, but now I might have a baby."
>
> 🌹 HIGH SCHOOL GIRL

Though the *Good Guy* may not be testing you just to see how much he can get away with, he's definitely still keeping an eye out for whether you respect yourself or not. And it will impact the future of your relationship.

> "I had sex with a girl I had been talking to her since before I got in the eighth grade... She had everything I wanted in a woman, but I don't think she respected herself as much as she thought. Her priorities were in line for the most part, except for her obsession with sex. She acted like all she had to offer me was her body, and I wanted to be with a girl who respected herself and wanted more from the relationship than sex."
>
> ~ HIGH SCHOOL GUY

It seems her lack of self-respect was the only thing he didn't like about her, and that was a deal breaker for him. It can also be a deal breaker for so many other guys.

The *Best Guy* would never put you through a test nor would he ever do anything to disrespect you. He's the guy who only dates girls who respect themselves and will end the relationship the minute he suspects you don't.

> "My girlfriend made it clear we won't be having sex in high school, and she knows I respect her. I would never pressure her into anything. Unlike most boys in high school, I realize how much good it does for a relationship to wait. We are making our relationship stronger by waiting and focusing on each other. I love the fact that she respects herself so much."
>
> ~ HIGH SCHOOL GUY

Even if this guy's girlfriend hadn't declared she intended to wait for sex, there are always clues a boy can detect to determine whether a girl respects herself.

The test:

If a guy is pressuring you for sex, this is a good sign he doesn't respect you. But this lack of respect doesn't just begin when he asks for sex. In most cases, he bases his lack of respect for you on signals he has already gotten from you through a series of subtle tests. From the moment they meet you, guys notice whether you respect yourself. Whether they admit it or not, while trying to determine your level of self-respect, many guys want to figure out how much they can get away with in a relationship. It's all part of the hunt or a calculated process to figure out how to get you to a point where he can get what he wants.

> *If a guy is pressuring you for sex, this is a good sign he doesn't respect you.*

When guys are testing your respect levels, they push your boundaries. The test typically begins with simply asking for what he wants. He will ask over and over until he is sure of your answer. The types of things he asks for and the level of intensity depends on the type of guy he is and the type of relationship you have with him. He may be blunt or subtle when he asks. But the purpose of asking is the same for all guys: to determine how far you will go to give him what he wants. You can determine what he thinks of you by listening to what he says. Red flags should go up every time you sense he expects you to give up something important to you for his own pleasure.

An example:

You have twenty dollars to buy a book you need and a guy asks you for ten dollars because he wants to buy a game. You may say no because that's all the money you have. You say it with a smile to be kind, but he doesn't hear what you said as much as he notices how you said it (i.e., you were smiling when you said it). Because you smiled, he thinks there's a chance of getting what he wants. So he continues to ask you for the money over and over. Note: If a guy continues to pressure you for something and disregards your first answer, this is a sign he might not respect you.

As a result of his continuing to ask, you give in and agree to give him the money even though you need it yourself. He saw you compromise your needs for his desires, and once you agree to give the first ten dollars, it sends the message he may be able to get more from you.

So he comes back again asking for more money from you until it's all gone. How did this happen? You thought you were just being kind, and if you gave in a little, he would stop asking. But you sent a nonverbal message your needs were not important. And if you and your needs aren't important to you, then why should they be important to anyone else?

When it comes to sex, a guy will do the same thing—ask. Some will be blunt and go for the shock value of asking for what he wants straight out, even if he barely knows you. But, the average guy will use three approaches to test to see if you are the kind of girl who is open for sex: the verbal test, the visual test and the touch test.

So, here are the details of the tests guys might put you through to see if you are "that kind of girl."

Green Light #1: Verbal Test

Usually the first test is the verbal test. They start talking to you about sex, telling you what others are doing, then they begin telling you what they want to do with you if they get a chance. They may do this even before they know you well. If a guy says something that sounds disrespectful to a girl, she may blow it off and think he must be joking or he's not serious. But when you entertain this vulgar conversation and don't demand that he watch his mouth, you've given him his first green light that he can disrespect you.

Green Light #2: Visual Test

Next comes the visual test. As he continues explicit conversation about sex, he'll escalate to asking you to expose your body. He'll boldly ask you for naked or half-naked pictures of yourself.

{ **71%** (Seven out of ten) of guys say a girl who has "sexted" (e.g., sent/posted nude or semi-nude images of herself electronically) is not girlfriend material. }

It doesn't sound like something you would do, until he "promises" he's the only one who will ever see these pictures. This will be something private and special between the two of you. Reluctantly, you send the picture. When you do, this continues to communicate to him you don't respect yourself. You desire to please him more than you desire to honor what you want or think is right. To you, this is a way to keep him happy without having sex, but he knows he just got the second green light.

> **! Note:** Anytime nudity of a person under the age of eighteen is shared electronically, both the sender and the receiver (if retained in his/her possession) are committing an illegal act. It's considered distribution and possession of child pornography.

Green Light #3: Touch Test

His third attempt is the touch test, and it usually doesn't take long for him to try. His hands start to roam to areas that should be private. You knock them away and tell him to stop. There may even be a smile on your face when saying it, which may make the guy question how serious you are. He retreats and waits a little while before he tries it again. Again you knock them away. You dance that dance back and forth a few times until you get tired of resisting and you allow his hands to stay. He wore you down. And now that he has passed another green light, he's getting more and more confident he'll achieve his final goal. You've provided clear signals to him you're the type of girl who lacks self-respect and self-esteem. The type of girl who doesn't demand others to respect her decisions either.

After the third green light, he's certain he'll be able to get sex from you. So, the pressure begins. He's bound and determined to cross the finish line. Although this may not have been what you wanted, you convince yourself it is because again you want to make him happy. So, you succumb to the pressure and agree to have sex.

Now, if you still don't believe guys lose respect long before sex happens, check out what this young man wrote:

> *"I have a girlfriend, and we have been dating for sixteen months. Things started getting physical during the summer and began to change the relationship. Luckily I*

noticed the change and I told her. I had actually stopped respecting her..."

~ HIGH SCHOOL GUY

This couple had not even had sex. Yet, the young man had stopped respecting his girlfriend because of how physical the relationship had become. This young man is definitely one of the *Good Guys*. What happened with this guy is what happens with a lot of guys. The more physical the relationship becomes, the more they lose respect for the girls. Most guys just don't tell the girls like he did.

It's important to talk to your boyfriend about respect. But remember what you learned in the last chapter, guys will tell you what you want to hear. Boys may say they'll respect you no matter what, but that could change, or they just may not want to tell you the truth. It's important to have your own standards for behavior so no one else can convince you to disrespect yourself.

> *It's important to have your own standards for behavior so no one else can convince you to disrespect yourself.*

These are some of the tests guys conduct to see how much a girl respects herself. I think it's time girls start conducting their own tests to find out how much respect guys have for them.

How can you tell if a guy respects you?

1 Does he respect your decisions?

secret three

> *"You taught me girls do have the power, and if the guys don't respect your decision, they don't respect you."*
>
> — Middle School Girl

First, ask yourself, "Does he respect and accept my decisions?" This doesn't just mean a decision not to have sex. It can also include decisions not to have sexual conversations, send a nude or semi-nude picture, let him touch you inappropriately, or do anything else you're not comfortable with. He may tell you that he can't help himself because you're so irresistible. If he tries to persuade you to do more than you want to do at any point in your relationship he's not respecting your decisions, and therefore not respecting you.

It's important to stop this disrespect as soon as it happens. The moment a guy treats you disrespectfully, you should look him straight in the eyes, without smiling and tell him clearly and confidently you are not okay with that. If you are firm when you say it, he'll go back and tell all his friends you don't allow any disrespect and you are not that kind of girl. That's the kind of respect girls should have for themselves and the kind of reputation all girls should be known for.

2 Does he treat you the way he would want someone to treat his future daughter?

> *"... I liked the analogy you used about how guys should treat their girlfriends like they would want someone to treat their daughter. I've had a couple of bad relationships where I wish those guys would've treated me like they wanted their daughter treated."*
>
> — High School Girl

This point about a boy treating you the way he would want someone to treat his future daughter is something that often comes up in one of my classroom exercises called the Staircase. When we do this in class, the boys are my best teaching tools because girls get to hear exactly what they're thinking, which helps make my point.

First, let's consider the following steps of progression that lead to sex:

> Eye contact
> > Conversation
> > > Hug
> > > > Holding Hands
> > > > > Short Kiss (peck on the cheek)
> > > > > > Long Kiss (on the lips, no tongue)
> > > > > > > French Kiss
> > > > > > > > Touching over clothes
> > > > > > > > > Touching under clothes
> > > > > > > > > > Sex

You could argue I don't have enough steps or I have too many or they are out of order, but for most people, these are the steps.

In class, I ask the guys how far they would go down the staircase with their girlfriend or the hottest girl in the school.

Some of the guys say they would go all the way to the bottom, if given the opportunity. There are always some respectful guys who say they would stop long before sex. Next, I ask the boys to imagine they are older, married and have a daughter who is the same age as their current girlfriend. After coming home one evening, they discover their daughter's boyfriend is visiting and they are in the living room alone. They decide to peep in to make sure her boyfriend is respecting their daughter but more importantly she is respecting herself. Which point on the steps of progression would they consider to be disrespectful to their daughter?

Many of them say anything past his arm around her is unacceptable. Almost all the guys will say anything past French kissing is disrespectful. Every now and then I will have a guy who'll say he would be okay with his daughter doing more than French kissing. The rest of the guys jump all over him, saying things like, "Dude, what's wrong with you? That's your daughter we're talking about. You're going to be a horrible parent." Remember, these are some of the same guys who also said they would go all the way to the bottom of the staircase with their girlfriends.

I point out to the guys that for many of them, the lines they drew for their girlfriends were much farther down the staircase than the lines they drew for their future daughters. The guys will admit, "It shows we're hypocrites. We have double standards." I probe at why they're willing to go farther with their girlfriends than they would want guys to go with their future daughters. One guy said, "Because daughters are permanent." A daughter is someone they care about forever, and ultimately want the best for. A girlfriend at this age to them is just temporary.

I asked this young man to consider his girlfriend also had a father who probably didn't want anyone disrespecting his daughter. The young man responded, "If her father had done his job, she wouldn't have let me go that far." At this point, most of the girls in the class exploded saying, "You can't blame that on her father. Maybe her father wasn't a part of her life. Her father can't be with her 24/7. What about your father doing his job?"

Even though these are fair objections, they're missing the bigger picture. Regardless of whether his father did his job or her father did his job, the young lady has to respect herself. She has to set and demand a certain level of respect and hold boys to that standard. This boy just showed he wasn't going to respect a young lady any more than she respects herself. Another guy said it this way, "Girls know they lose more from being sexually active than we do. If they don't care, why should we care more about them than they care about themselves?"

Thankfully, this Staircase activity usually helps guys understand the problem with this line of thinking.

> *"The Staircase exercise has influenced the way I think. If I want my future daughter to not travel too far on that staircase, I need to respect the parents of the girls I date right now and not take their daughters too far down the staircase..."*
>
> ~High School Guy

Most guys aren't aware of how wrong this behavior is because it has become the norm for most teenagers. But, just because it's the norm doesn't mean they can't make a different and better choice. I tell young men in the classroom I'm waiting for a generation of young men to rise up who will respect girls even when girls don't respect themselves. It always warms my heart when the guys raise their hands to say they are "that guy."

> *"This presentation opened up my eyes about the real reason girls have sex at such a young age. I always thought girls were just loose. I never sat down to think sex might just be a replacement for love, attention or a*

> sense of self-worth some girls never received or had. I learned if a girl does not respect herself enough to say no, then it may be because she is emotionally broken and needs someone to love and respect her enough to say no, even when she won't. Your presentation changed me and the way I look at girls now. I now show them the respect every girl deserves, and I treat them how I would want another man to treat my future daughters. Thank you for teaching me this valuable lesson. I would not have thought the same without it."
>
> ~ High School Guy

The young man who wrote this letter understood the relationship between respect and sex. I applaud him for making the decision to respect women even when they won't respect themselves. But until I can get an entire generation of respectful guys to rise up, I'm going to need young ladies to demand the respect they deserve.

3. Does he allow you to do things that will make him lose respect for you down the road?

> "These girls need to have more self-respect. A couple of girls tried to make deals with me, thinking if they gave me oral sex or had sex with me, then I would go out with them, but I turned it down because I have sense."
>
> ~ High School Guy

Even if you decide not to have sex with a boy, other sexual acts like oral sex are just as disrespectful. If we discussed oral sex in class fourteen years ago, girls would blush or their eyes would get as big as quarters. Now, it seems to have become much more casual because girls often ask in class if it's a safe alternative to vaginal sex. Recently, I had a disturbing discussion in a class of eighth-grade girls. The young ladies asked me what they could do to make boys like them if they shouldn't have sex. One girl suggested oral sex. After I explained to her oral sex is sex, I told them they don't have to do anything to make a boy like them. They are the prize. Any boy worth having will like a girl because of who she is, not because of what she will do for him.

Unfortunately, this conversation isn't so surprising. So many young ladies base their decisions on what a boy wants rather than what they want. Many girls act as if their sole purpose is to please guys and make them happy. This mentality must change. Every girl has a purpose in life much greater than pleasing guys or getting guys to like them. My hope is that if you don't know yours, you will work harder on finding out what that purpose is.

> *Every girl has a purpose in life much greater than pleasing guys or getting guys to like them.*

Getting back to oral sex, I've often wondered how guys were able to get girls to perform oral sex so easily. Only to find out in a lot of cases, a guy doesn't have to do anything because oral sex is the girl's idea. The girls, like the eighth-grade girls mentioned before, are trying to do whatever they think will make guys like them. And yet, a lot of girls don't even know how guys feel about girls who will perform oral sex. Once, a boy told an entire class if a girl will perform oral sex on him, he'll never look at her the same way. He admitted to allowing girls to do it, and specified he just doesn't respect them afterward. He also said he definitely won't kiss them afterward because it's disgusting.

secret three

The secret this young man just revealed is oral sex can definitely cause guys to lose respect for a girl. Yet, many young women seem to think it will make guys like them more.

Aside from the desire for guys to like them, girls also offer oral sex in place of vaginal sex as a way to remain a virgin and avoid physical consequences. Even though they won't get pregnant, they don't realize they are still at risk of contracting STDs and experiencing negative emotional consequences.

> "I never realized the lack of respect I had for myself. I'm still a virgin. But, I've hooked up [performed oral sex], and it has screwed up my life. I thought if I hooked up with the last two guys I dated they would like me more. The first guy after it was all over was like, 'I hope we can be friends.' The second guy said the same thing after a few months. After we hooked up, he never talked to me again and told the whole school what I did. This has affected me emotionally and made me feel like crap."
>
> — High School Girl

This young lady made poor sexual decisions to make guys like her. But, she had to face the sad reality; guys who had no intention of being in a long-term relationship with her were just using and disrespecting her. Even though she avoided pregnancy and STDs—this time—she wasn't able to escape the emotional consequences, which can be just as devastating as the physical ones.

4 Does he have the same standards for you he'd have for a future wife?

When young ladies don't respect themselves now, those decisions can affect them in later relationships. Check out a conversation I had with one of my married friends about his standards when deciding to marry his wife, Chloe.

CASE STUDY
Phillip and Chloe

Phillip: Before I got married, I always had a number in my head of the maximum number of sexual partners a woman could have in order for me to marry her. If Chloe's number had been higher than that, I wouldn't have married her.

Me: Did you have a maximum number for the women you dated?

Phillip: No.

Me: Had your number of previous sexual partners exceeded the limit you set for your future wife?

Phillip: Of course it had.

Me: That's crazy and hypocritical. How could you expect your future wife to live up to a standard you couldn't even meet?

Phillip: Because she should have had more respect for herself than that.

> **Me:** Wait a minute. You weren't respecting yourself when you were racking up your number of sexual partners. You also weren't concerned about your girlfriends respecting themselves when you were dating them.
>
> **Phillip:** That's because my standards were much higher when I selected my wife than they were when I picked my girlfriends. I didn't have to respect a woman to have sex with her, but I refused to marry a woman I didn't respect. Chloe was the woman I wanted to spend the rest of my life with. This is the woman that would be my wife and the mother of my children.

I shared the above story in a class one day. A twenty-six-year-old was substitute teaching that day. When the students left the class, the substitute teacher told me she wished she had been able to share her personal story. She was getting married in a couple of months, and she was a virgin. There were two young men who broke up with her in high school because she wouldn't have sex with them. She found it interesting that in the previous six months, both of those young men had gone to great lengths to try to find her. When they were ready to get married, they went looking for the girl from high school that respected herself enough to say no to sex.

I'm not saying if you don't have sex now, all the guys you turn down today will want to marry you when you get older. However, guys will respect you if you respect yourself, and respect is important in a potential marriage. But, young ladies, you should make the decision to respect yourselves for one reason only: You are valuable . . . period!

they won't respect you if you don't respect yourself

Why don't girls always demand respect?

1 Denial is a wonderful thing—temporarily.

> "I just want to thank you for coming to the school and opening my eyes. I was one of those girls that was in denial about sex, but not anymore . . . When I heard my boyfriend say in class that he wouldn't want a guy having sex with his future daughter as a teenager because that would be disrespectful, I was crushed. I couldn't understand why he didn't think he was disrespecting me when we had sex. From now on I will demand that he treats me with the same respect he wants for his future daughter. If not, we're done."
>
> — HIGH SCHOOL GIRL

Some young ladies don't think sex and respect have anything to do with each other, and thus don't see having sex as disrespecting themselves. In fact, when guys in class say they don't respect girls who have sex with them, the girls all argue it's not true, and tell them they can't speak for all guys.

I agree they can't speak for all guys, but guys do have insight on how other guys think. Instead of immediately shutting the guys down, those young ladies should have listened. They were blessed to get the inside scoop on guys from guys.

I understand why girls get so angry with guys. If a young lady is having sex with her boyfriend and she hears a guy in class say guys don't respect girls who have sex with them, she has one of two choices:

1. She can accept the fact she is being disrespected, confront her boyfriend, quit having sex and risk losing him.

2. She can believe her boyfriend is different from all the guys in the class and continue to have sex with him . . . and probably realize later she was being disrespected.

Unfortunately, far too many girls choose the second option. But why would girls choose to live in denial about respect? It may be because they see so many other girls and women being disrespected and objectified in the media, whether in music videos, on reality TV shows, pornography, or in real life. It seems that disrespect has become expected, common and acceptable.

For example, several years ago there was a case involving a popular entertainer who assaulted his equally popular girlfriend. Whenever this story was discussed in class, many girls argued the woman must have done something to deserve the abuse. It's unbelievable how many young ladies came to the man's defense, supporting him in spite of his actions. And all because they thought he was so good looking, as though looks compensate for a lack of respect. What's worse, the girlfriend said she still loved him and they were seen in public together a year or so later. She was disrespected in the worst way, and yet denied it for "love."

I wish more girls understood they hold the power. You can and should demand respect from guys. Sadly, many girls would rather have something else, which I've identified in the next section.

2 Girls would rather be liked than respected.

> "I am in eighth grade and my boyfriend is a senior in high school. We talk on the phone, and I tell him if we get a chance, I want to have sex with him. I know he

will not respect me after it is over. I just feel like I have to have sex with him to make him stay."

                              Middle School Girl

Wow. How sad is this? She knows he won't respect her after sex, but thinks she doesn't have a choice if she wants him to stay with her. It's disheartening her logic is this flawed at such a young age. If she doesn't correct her thinking soon, she'll end up an adult woman making poor relationship choices just to keep a man.

Yes, guys may like you (or rather what you do for them) temporarily and stick around a little longer if you have sex with them. They won't, however, respect you more because you did. I've never heard a guy say, "Yeah, my girlfriend gives it up every Friday night, and I really respect her for that." But I have heard guys say, "I've been trying to get my girlfriend to have sex for six months and she hasn't given in. Even though I got upset with her, I had to respect her because at least she was strong enough to hold her ground." You'll get much more respect for saying no than you ever will for saying yes.

> *You'll get much more respect for saying no than you ever will for saying yes.*

"I decided to tell my boyfriend if he really loves me and thinks we are going to last forever, he could wait until we get married to have sex. He told me he respects me a lot more now since I was able to say no and not just do it because he wanted to do it."

                              High School Girl

Many girls believe all guys want to be with the girls who are willing to do whatever they ask. Yet, many guys respect a woman who has her own mind and is strong enough to stick with her convictions. They often find those girls more attractive.

> **71%** (three out of four) of guys say they have more respect for girls who say no to sex.

"Once I sat down and thought about the consequences, my girlfriend and I came to the decision to put sex down until marriage. She brought the idea of waiting up, and it changed my whole outlook on her character. It's easier to respect a female who can say, 'Let's wait.' than one who'll give in."

— HIGH SCHOOL GUY

It's great to see some girls get it. I'm so happy to be able to end this section with a letter from a young lady who realized how important it is to have respect.

"January 1 will make the one-year anniversary for me and my boyfriend. That's when we were supposed to start having sex, but after your first day of class I told him I changed my mind and I wanted to be abstinent. He respected it but didn't like it at all. At first he said, 'No way am I being abstinent.' But he sort of lightened up now. I don't think he thinks I'm serious. Even though this is the guy I pictured kids and a future with, I'm preparing myself emotionally for a breakup just in case he leaves me when he realizes I'm serious. But if he leaves me, I know he will leave me with respect."

— HIGH SCHOOL GIRL

Isn't it wonderful this young lady knows what she deserves? She was even willing to sacrifice what was most likely a temporary relationship to get it. Unfortunately, this doesn't happen as much as it should. But guess what? It's not too late to begin building respect for yourself, no matter what has happened in the past.

> *It's not too late to begin building respect for yourself, no matter what has happened in the past.*

Respect—starting over

> *"I'm ashamed of myself for how many times I let a guy disrespect me and my body or just the fact that I didn't respect my own body."*
>
> — High School Girl

After reading this, you may have realized you haven't been respecting yourself. If so, you may not be quite sure how to start. The good news is it's not too late.

To start, you must begin by loving yourself. The first question to ask is, "Do I love myself?" If you recall from Chapter 1, love means you will always do what's best for someone and not harm him or her. Given this definition, recognize your own worth and set a new standard for how you should be treated. Understand you deserve to be treated with the utmost respect by yourself and by others. When you feel as if that new standard is being violated, don't allow it, and know when to walk away.

> *"What you told us about respecting ourselves so much that we don't have sex confused me at first. But as you explained it, it gradually seemed more and more and*

more logical: I should like myself enough that a boy's approval of me or desire for me shouldn't matter."

— HIGH SCHOOL GIRL

Below are several practical steps you can take to start rebuilding your self-respect.

1. Make sure to carry yourself in a way that demonstrates you honor yourself. You do this by the way you dress, the way you talk, the places you go and the company you keep.
2. Set boundaries for how far you will go in a relationship and stick to them.
3. If you're in a relationship where you are currently sexually active, take a stand with your boyfriend. If he truly loves you, he may not like it, but he'll respect your decision.
4. Consider taking a break from dating and focus on loving and respecting yourself, and becoming the best person you can be.
5. Be selective of the media you consume. Don't watch shows or listen to music where young ladies are disrespecting themselves or being disrespected.

they won't respect you if you don't respect yourself

As I shared at the beginning of this chapter, any guy who will pressure you to have sex does not respect you. Far too often, I hear the following statement from girls: "I won't say he raped me. I just didn't want to have sex." There's the girl who says no, but her no is ignored; then there's the girl who feels no, but she doesn't say it. Either way, when the sex is over, they both feel violated. They both were pressured/forced to do something they didn't want to do and that is WRONG! Let me be clear, even if a guy doesn't think a girl respects herself, it NEVER gives him a right to pressure/force her to have sex.

Rape is NEVER the fault of the person who was assaulted.

Now that you know . . .

If you put your own worth before his pleasure and say no to sex, he will recognize you as a girl who respects herself and has her head on straight. If you falter or compromise your values, he'll push the limits to see how far you'll go. If you lower your standards to make him happy, he'll only lose interest because he won't respect you. Even if he stays for sex, that doesn't mean he thinks you're the right one, you're just the one for right now. Bottom line, you have to know your worth and refuse to settle for less. When it comes to respect, he won't if you don't.

> "Before you came, it's not that I didn't value myself, it's that I didn't value myself the way I should. I see now that if someone doesn't respect my decision to be celibate, then he doesn't deserve me."
>
> — HIGH SCHOOL GIRL

SECRET 4

Sex changes things.

"After I had sex with my ex-girlfriend, I could never look at her the same way. It's like I couldn't trust her anymore. Since she agreed to have sex with me, how could I be sure she wasn't having sex with someone else as well? I know that doesn't make sense because she could have the same question about me, but I think it's common for guys to think like this. I think our relationship would have lasted longer if we hadn't had sex."

~ High School Guy

PLAYER	GOOD GUY	BEST GUY
After he gets sex, he has reached his goal, and he's ready for another challenge.	He may be just as shocked as you are that sex changes the relationship. Once he notices the change, he either tries to get out or he discontinues sex.	You don't have to worry about sex changing the relationship with him because he's committed to abstaining from sex.

secret four

To uncover this secret, I had to do some digging because even though guys say it happens, they don't always know why. The bottom line is once most guys have sex with you, they feel differently about you, as the letter above reflects.

> "Once I felt loved and special [by my ex-boyfriend], I was happy and thought he was perfect; until I made the mistake of giving my virginity to him. Once he knew he had me, the love and happiness was no longer seen. To all the girls out there that think being sexually active will give you love and attention, it doesn't. It just causes you more problems."
>
> —High School Girl

It's easy to assume this young lady may have been dating a *Player*. After he got what he wanted, he no longer felt the need to make her feel loved and special. But don't think sex only changes things when you're dating a *Player*. It can change things even when you're dating a *Good Guy*.

> "The whole discussion opened up my eyes to things more important than sex in a relationship. I have been with my girlfriend for almost a year now, and we had started having sex. But we noticed it complicated our relationship, and we weren't ready for that. Then you came and spoke, and it helped me say to myself, 'I will never do that again until marriage.'"
>
> —High School Guy

We can tell he is a *Good Guy* because, once he noticed sex was complicating the relationship, he was willing to sacrifice

sex changes things

pleasure for the greater good of a long-term relationship. The only way to avoid these complications altogether is to date one of the *Best Guys*, who is committed to abstaining from sex in his relationships. Believe me, there are plenty of them out there.

Having sex is a bigger decision than your peers and the media may have you believe. You need to be mature enough to handle everything that goes along with this behavior. Let's look at some of the other issues you'll have to deal with in the relationship once you start having sex:

- What will he expect about the frequency of sex now that you've had it?
- What will you do if a pregnancy happens?
- How will you feel if others find out you've had sex?
- How will it feel to see him with someone else if the relationship ends?
- Does he care about you or does he just want the sex?

Considering all the above factors, it's hard to see how things would not change after sex. The nicest, most considerate, loyal guy in the world will not keep you from having to deal with the above issues if you're sexually active.

What changes?

Guys' feelings and expectations

"I was dating this girl, and I was very interested in her before we had sex; now I feel less interested in her than I was before. I like her still, but I don't feel the same way I felt before."

~ HIGH SCHOOL GUY

secret four

The letter above is typical of what I hear from a lot of guys about sex. Many times they can't put their finger on why their feelings change or why they lose interest. They just know they feel differently about the girl after sex.

Some guys can easily pinpoint why they no longer want to be with a girl they've had sex with. As you might guess, the *Players* usually know why their feelings change after sex—they got what they wanted and they've completed the challenge. The *Good Guys* are the ones who may not understand exactly what happens because they weren't expecting the change in feelings at all.

> "In relationships, the way you feel about one another is great until you have sex. It seems the way you felt before was better than the way after. I guess what I'm trying to say is when you get in a physical relationship, the feelings you have for one another change because of what you did."
>
> ~ HIGH SCHOOL GUY

If these *Good Guys* don't understand why and how the feelings change, then how could you be expected to understand either? In the next section, we'll take a look at why.

Why the change?

Guys have told me their feelings can change for four reasons.

1. It's no longer a challenge because they've gotten the prize.
2. Girls become clingy.

3. They want to experience sexual pleasure with other girls.
4. They are stressed due to potential physical consequences.

1 It's no longer a challenge because they've gotten the prize.

> "Before you came and talked to us, I viewed sex as the goal; and then once I had gotten it, I would just leave. Now I see how wrong I was. I have a lot of regrets about the decisions I have made."
>
> ~ HIGH SCHOOL GUY

The *Player* is normally the type of guy who believes relationships are no longer a challenge after sex. Sex for him is just like playing a video game. Once he reaches the targeted level, the thrill is over, and he's now trying to get to the next level. He likes the challenge and enjoys the thrill of the pursuit. Once he achieves his goal and the initial sexual experience is over, the pursuit is no longer necessary. So, even if he continues to have sex with her, in the back of his mind he's already looking for the challenge of the next pursuit.

It's important to understand my next point. Guys' feelings will change after sex because they know they've captured the prize. But when I refer to the "prize," it's not my intent to imply you are just a sexual being. There is so much more to you than your body. For young boys in relationships, often sex or your body is their ultimate goal if they don't value you for who you are as a person. In that case, to them, sex is the prize.

A guy in one of my classes gave the following reason for why he believes a guy's feelings change after sex. "Because once

secret four

you have sex with her, you've already gotten all of her. There's nothing left to look forward to." This may sound strange and even cold, but let's consider the following scenario.

Don't give your best gift first.

> *There is so much more to you than your body.*

Imagine your parents gave you your biggest and best Christmas present on Thanksgiving Day. You loved it and played with it often. Now imagine it's Christmas Day and everyone is getting great gifts. If you got your biggest and best gift a month ago, would you be as excited about the smaller presents you open on Christmas morning? Better yet, would you still be excited about the gift you got a month ago? I seriously doubt it. Opening gifts on Christmas Day is now a letdown. It's anti-climactic. If you give your body (and the emotional attachment that comes with sex), which is your most valuable possession to your boyfriend now, what do either of you have to look forward to later?

> *"I thought the last guy I dated loved me, but when he broke up with me a month after we started having sex, I realized all he wanted was my body. Hearing you speak made me value myself and made me understand my body is mine and mine only, and I'll never again give it to someone who doesn't deserve it."*
>
> — HIGH SCHOOL GIRL

Many of you will agree the boys you meet now are not the guys you will marry. Why give something so precious to

sex changes things

someone who you already know is just a temporary relationship in your life? Some girls don't see it this way, but let's look at the following lottery ticket analogy.

> If you won a thousand dollars, five hundred or even one hundred dollars in the lottery, would you give it to your boyfriend?
>
> Ninety-nine percent of girls will say no. I find it interesting few girls would give as little as one hundred dollars to their boyfriends if they won the lottery. Yet, many of those girls have already given their bodies to them. What does this say about the value young women place on their bodies? Not much. This is essentially saying, "My boyfriend can't have one hundred dollars, but he can have my body whenever he asks for it."
>
> Young ladies, if you give one hundred dollars to your boyfriend and you break up, five years from now you won't worry about that money. But, if you give your body to your boyfriend, and the relationship ends, five years from now, you could still be paying a huge price for that decision.

Why give something so precious to someone who you already know is just a temporary relationship in your life?

Many young ladies declare it's okay to have sex with their boyfriends since they believe they are going to get married. What these young ladies need to understand is so much can happen between now and the time they plan to get married. Between middle/high school and marriage, you'll mature. Your interests will change. As teenagers, you have little control over your lives since your parents are making most of the major life decisions.

In all probability, you're dating someone now who you'll refer to in the future as your ex. On the rare occasion you do stay together for the long run, you should consider the above Christmas present analogy. As a teenager, if you begin having sex early, the sex might not be as meaningful after a while.

> *In all probability, you're dating someone now who you'll refer to in the future as your ex.*

"I am not a virgin. I don't regret who I had sex with, but I do regret when I had sex. I had sex too early. I was sixteen, and I made an adult decision to have sex. I have no bad story about my first time. I'm actually still with the guy, but our relationship isn't as meaningful as I wish it were. Sometimes the act of sex is just equal to what a kiss used to be."

— High School Girl

She seems to attribute the fact that her relationship isn't as meaningful to the fact that they started having sex when they were too young. Now, sex for them has become as common as a kiss. Do you want this to be your experience?

2 Girls become clingy.

Sex can also change a relationship by making girls "clingy" afterward. This attachment is the result of a real physiological reaction that occurs with sex. During sex, a hormone or chemical called oxytocin, known as the bonding hormone, is released and causes a woman to bond with her partner. It is also released in women's brains on at least two other occasions: during childbirth and breastfeeding. Studies now show small amounts of oxytocin can be released with any amount of touching, such as holding hands, kissing, etc. It seems logical that physical touch would cause you to feel closer to another person.

Think about how a girl's clinginess impacts the *Player*. Oxytocin is also released in a guy's brain, just in lesser amounts. If he starts to feel more attached to her as a result of the sex, it scares him because he wasn't ever planning to commit to this girl. He starts to back away because he feels suffocated and knows they may end up in a relationship he never wanted.

A *Good Guy* may find his girlfriend's clinginess after sex more than he wants to deal with as well.

> "You said a lot of things I could easily relate to—like how girls and guys feel toward one another and the oxytocin chemical that's released with sex. I was recently in a relationship with a girl, and we were having sex. No matter what I did, she just liked me more and more. I hate clingy girls, but I'm not a heartbreaker either. So I gradually stopped showing interest in her so she would see I wasn't the greatest guy in the world and lighten up on the emotions or find someone else."
>
> ~ HIGH SCHOOL GUY

Here you have a guy who's questioning why a girl continues to like him even though he wasn't giving her the best treatment. Since he's not a heartbreaker, most girls would probably see him as a *Good Guy*. In this case, even the *Good Guy* backed away

secret four

from the relationship because of her clinginess. I bet the girl had no idea why. Once again, sex changes things.

Oxytocin also causes girls to trust a person, even if he isn't trustworthy. Many girls stay in relationships with guys who have cheated on them because they "just can't get him out of their system." Whenever a girl says this, I can almost guarantee she has been sexually active with the young man. Oxytocin clouds judgment.

> *"After sex I found myself not respecting me as much. I became clingy and started to hold on even when things got bad, but not anymore."*
>
> — HIGH SCHOOL GIRL

I have found that girls who are sexually active often accept more emotional, physical, verbal and sexual abuse from their boyfriends than girls who aren't.

I have found that girls who are sexually active often accept more emotional, physical, verbal and sexual abuse from their boyfriends than girls who aren't. They often end up staying in an abusive relationship longer with a person they've had sex with than they would a person they haven't. They typically do this because they don't want to admit they made a mistake and had sex with the wrong person. As a result, they try much harder to make the wrong person the right one.

3 **They want to experience sexual pleasure with other girls.**

Even though I learned these secrets from guys years ago, I try to confirm the secrets every chance I get. So, every time I go to a new school, I continue to ask guys the questions in this book. I never know when a guy may add a twist to one of the secrets that would be beneficial for you to know. And that's exactly what happened when I had the following conversation with a class:

> **Me:** Guys told me at another school that once they have sex with a girl, their feelings for her change. Do you think that's true?
>
> **Most of the male students:** Yes
>
> **Me:** Why do you think that's the case?
>
> **Male student:** Sex makes you want to cheat.
>
> **Me:** Well, I've never heard that before. How does sex make you want to cheat?
>
> **Male student:** Well, it did for me anyway. I was fourteen when I lost my virginity to my fifteen-year-old girlfriend, and she was the one who pressured me to have sex. I loved the sex, and after I had sex that first time, I wanted it all the time. Then I got curious and started wondering whether sex would feel the same with every girl, so I decided to find out. But, I feel like it's my girlfriend's fault that I cheated on her because she's the one who pressured me to have

> sex. If I hadn't had sex with her, we might still be together and I might still be a virgin. She's the one who turned me on to sex.

Young ladies, you must understand that sex as a teenager does more damage to your relationship than you might imagine. In fact, it often does more to increase the guy's willingness to be unfaithful than it does to strengthen your relationship with him.

> *"I lost my virginity my sophomore year with my ex, who I dated for nine months. I waited until the ninth month to have sex because I was 'in love,' and two weeks later he left me because he wanted that feeling from every girl."*
>
> — HIGH SCHOOL GIRL

4. They are stressed due to potential physical consequences.

It's easy to have a positive relationship as long as everything is going great. But stress has a way of making even the cutest, most popular couple in school question whether they belong together. Unfortunately, teenagers don't always realize how much stress comes with sex. In the heat of the moment, the negative consequences that may result from sex may be the farthest thing from your minds. But they still do exist. It's often difficult for the relationship to survive a negative physical consequence like pregnancy or an STD.

sex changes things

I spoke to a young man once who admitted sex ruined his last relationship. He said his girlfriend had a pregnancy scare. The period of time between thinking she may be pregnant and finding out she wasn't was extremely stressful for both of them. They couldn't agree on what to do if she actually was pregnant, and it put a lot of strain on their relationship.

Think about some things you'd have to deal with if you found out you were pregnant:

- What decision will you make about the baby? (Note: Every decision comes with its own consequence.)
- How are you going to tell your parents, and how will they react?
- How can you afford to take care of a baby when you don't have jobs?
- How will this affect your social lives and ability to participate in extracurricular activities?
- Will you be able to graduate high school and go to college?

These are questions that may not go through your mind in the heat of the moment. But they can definitely change things afterward.

Even after finding out his girlfriend wasn't pregnant, the young man said so much arguing had taken place that they just parted ways. He said if they'd never had sex, they might still be dating.

Pregnancy is only one of the consequences that can cause stress and complications in a relationship. Can you imagine the conversations that take place when one partner contracts an STD?

secret four

> "Recently I found out I got chlamydia while with my boyfriend. Of course his first reaction was to accuse me and call me 'dirty' and 'nasty.' We both don't know who had it first, or how one of us even got it. After all we went through, we broke up."
>
> — HIGH SCHOOL GIRL

What would be your first reaction if you were diagnosed with an STD in (what you thought was) a monogamous relationship? You would probably assume the other person cheated on you. In fact, certain STDs can lay dormant in the body for years without causing noticeable symptoms. Your partner could have contracted the STD before you started dating him and just not have known. This young lady brings up a good point when she says neither of them knows who contracted the STD first. The uncertainty would definitely be enough to strain the trust between them. It's difficult for a relationship to survive accusations of unfaithfulness whenever one partner contracts an STD.

In fact, certain STDs can lay dormant in the body for years without causing noticeable symptoms.

As a teenager, you should spend your time and energy on things that will help you become successful as an adult. Instead, once you introduce sex, both of you become preoccupied and concerned with these issues and complications, which could be potentially life changing.

sex changes things

What happens as a result of the changed feelings/expectations?

1 Friendships are destroyed.

Over fourteen years of speaking to teens, I've been most surprised by how often girls have sex with guys they consider best friends. They aren't dating. They're just friends. Do girls really believe something this intimate won't change the friendship? The common notion today is sex is just sex and you should be able to have it and "not catch feelings." But in reality, this rarely happens, despite what you might see in movies like *No Strings Attached*.

A girl may decide to have sex with her friend for several reasons. She may just want to know what sex feels like, no longer want to be a virgin by a certain age or want to have sex with someone she trusts. But sure enough because of the oxytocin, her feelings change, and she wants more from the guy than just sex. She wants a relationship. But the guy is now feeling awkward. This wasn't their original agreement, and he no longer wants to be around someone who's pressuring him for more. He didn't sign up for a long-term relationship, and now they both lose out on a good friendship that was supposed to be worth saving.

Saving girls from themselves . . .

Thank goodness there are some *Best Guys* out there who'll save girls from themselves when they aren't thinking clearly. I'll never forget one young lady who came to thank me for speaking to the class. Her best friend since elementary school was a guy. She said she'd asked him to have sex with her just so she could see what sex was like. She felt it would be best to share that experience with someone she knew well and could trust. He refused.

She was hurt when he turned her down because she thought it meant he didn't find her attractive. It wasn't until she heard me speak that she realized he turned her down because of his love and respect for her, not because he didn't find her attractive. Once she understood, she was grateful he hadn't agreed to have sex with her.

I'm glad this story ended well. But, it still concerns me that this girl interpreted his refusal to have sex as a rejection based on her attractiveness. Too often, girls equate sex with feeling pretty, being wanted or desired.

> "My first time was not that special, 'cause we dated for like a week, had sex, and he broke up with me the next day. I was hurt, and I know it was the wrong thing to do, but I did feel pretty and loved at the time."
>
> HIGH SCHOOL GIRL

It's important to notice what this young lady does and doesn't say about how sex made her feel. She doesn't say she believed this guy loved her—after all, they had only been dating for a week. She said she felt loved at the time. You should never risk your health and future to feel good about yourself. Real love never requires that.

I wish more young ladies based their value on their futures and their potential rather than on whether a guy finds them attractive or wants to have sex.

2 Relationships fall apart sooner.

> "I lost my virginity when I was fifteen years old to a boy I had dated for a year. It was one of the worst mistakes I've ever made in my life. It was awkward, uncomfortable, and scary. We broke up two months later. Our relationship completely fell apart after we had sex. I wouldn't recommend it to anyone."
>
> — High School Girl

When reading letters from young ladies whose relationships ended after being sexually active with their boyfriends, I began to notice an interesting pattern. I saw letter after letter that read something like this: "We had been together XX number of months/years before we started having sex . . . we broke up X days/months after we had sex." Girls often believe having sex with their boyfriends will make the boyfriends stay in the relationship longer. Unfortunately, that isn't how it actually plays out in real life. Could it be sex simply marks the beginning of the end?

> "I lost my virginity at fourteen with my boyfriend of a year and five months . . . A month after we had sex he broke up with me."
>
> — High School Girl

> "The morning I lost my virginity was the morning my boyfriend told me it was over."
>
> — High School Girl

secret four

> "I lost my virginity when I was fifteen to a boy I had been with for nine months at that time... We broke up a few months later."
>
> — HIGH SCHOOL GIRL

I receive far too many letters that share the same pattern as the letters above. Time together before sex is typically longer than time together after sex.

I often wonder whether these young ladies would've been so eager or willing to have sex with their boyfriends if they'd known how soon the relationship was going to end afterward.

Time together before sex is typically longer than time together after sex.

We talked about this in class one day, and a young lady shared a story about her male friend. He dated a girl for two years who was a virgin, and he had no problem being in the relationship without sex. They became sexually active after two years, and he broke up with her within a month or so of them having sex. She couldn't understand how he'd stayed with a girl for two years without sex and then broken up with her so soon after. He explained, "I thought she was different than most girls. When she had sex with me, I realized she was just like all the other girls who will have sex with guys." He thought she had a higher standard.

Wow. Are guys really that hypocritical? It's wrong for a guy to pursue a girl, and then judge her after she agrees to do something he wanted (and did himself). Unfortunately, that's often the reality.

Of course, you're smart enough to stay away from guys who have a reputation of breaking up with girls shortly after having sex. But you need to know an accelerated breakup could happen with any guy. Does a *Good Guy* go into a relationship planning for it to end shortly after he gets sex from the girl? Probably not. Yet, the intense emotions attached to sex can often be difficult for any guy to deal with, leading him to check out of the relationship.

> "I lost my virginity to a girl in August and everything changed. We had been friends for two years before we started dating . . . After we had sex, I didn't take pride in it like any other male would. If anything, I felt different because at that point I knew I didn't 'love' her like I used to. And I'm not trying to sound like a jerk, but it just wasn't there . . . A few months later, we even stopped being friends . . . Being a virgin as a senior actually felt great, but I can't be a proud virgin anymore. All I can do is regret the loss of it and move on."
>
> ~High School Guy

Is it you or the sex?

> "I've only had sex with one guy my whole life. Our relationship is off and on, but no matter what we always go back to each other. I'm not sure if it's the sex or love that brings us back together. This time I want to make it count and actually know. I'm planning on removing sex from our relationship and seeing if it's meant to be."
>
> ~High School Girl

When a girl tells me she's having sex with her boyfriend, but not to worry because their relationship is built on love, trust and respect and not sex, I'm not surprised to hear that declaration. Isn't that what every girl believes? But can a girl ever really know in her teen years what he truly feels about her? Once sex is introduced, the relationship can become primarily physical. When you're together, you're either having sex or talking about having sex. You convince yourself he'd be with you even if you weren't having sex. In the back of your mind, you're always wondering whether he's dating you because of who you are or because of what you're giving him. The only way to be sure he's not only with you for sex is to remove it from the equation entirely.

One way to tell: the Thirty-Days Test.

One way for young ladies to determine whether their boyfriends are with them because of the sex is to try the thirty-days test.

Stop all physical contact, including hugging and kissing, with your boyfriend for thirty days and then reflect on the status of your relationship.

Many girls find that by day thirty, they're no longer in a relationship. When they remove the physical contact from the relationship, they realize they didn't have a lot to talk about and had little in common. This also plays out in same-sex relationships.

> "I was recently in a relationship for one-and-a-half years. We had sex nonstop. I thought it was okay or safer because she was just like me, a female. I couldn't get pregnant but was ignorant of the STDs I could still get. She loved me no doubt and I loved her, but sex ruined our relationship. We had little to discuss outside of sex."
>
> — HIGH SCHOOL GIRL

Check out a conversation I had in class one day with a young lady who wanted to put her boyfriend to the test:

> **Her:** Even though I know my boyfriend isn't there just for the sex, I want to put him to the test. So how can I tell him I want to stop having sex?
>
> **Me:** Just tell him everything you've heard in class over the past two days, and then see what he says. Don't let him know you're testing him though. Tell him you want the two of you to get to know each other in ways other than just the physical.
>
> **Her:** Okay, I'm going to do it.
>
> **Me (next day in class):** Hey, how'd it go last night? How did your boyfriend respond to the test?
>
> **Her:** He said he respected my decision. But since we'd already had sex, he thought it would be difficult to continue dating without it. So he just wants to take a break from the relationship for a while. I was not happy. I've invested two years into the relationship. And something as simple as taking sex off the table was all it took for him to walk away. I guess it was just a physical relationship after all.
>
> **Me:** It was probably only a matter of time before the relationship ended anyway. Be glad you found out before you had to deal with any physical consequences of sex.

secret four

When she left class the first day to go talk with him, she was so confident it wouldn't be a big deal for him to stop having sex for thirty days. After all, she wasn't asking him to give up sex forever—just thirty days. I'm sure that told her a lot about what he valued most about the relationship. I tried to console her after class because I could see how devastated her boyfriend's response left her. I'm hoping the experience will lead her to make wiser choices in future relationships.

Maybe an "every day" test would be better than the thirty-day test. Challenge your boyfriend to date you without sex every day and not just for thirty days. If he's up to the challenge, you can always be sure he's in the relationship with you based on who you are rather than what you may be giving him or will give him in a matter of days. If not, he's failed the test and it's time to move on.

You should also know that it's much easier to set this standard before you have sex than it is to change it after you've begun having sex.

> Challenge your boyfriend to date you without sex every day and not just for thirty days.

Now that you know . . .

Until now, you may not have thought sex could change a relationship—or maybe you thought it would change things for the better. Now you can see sex comes with many complicating factors that can have a serious impact on your relationship. Seriously consider if sex is worth all the mental, emotional and physical changes we've covered. If you have a great relationship without sex, that means someone cares about you for who you are and not what you can give him—why change that at all?

> "This past year I started dating this guy. We went out for a year and a half, and we broke up this summer before he went off to college. While we were in the relationship we had sex. We were both virgins before this. Then our conversations changed to how to have safe sex and what we would do if we got pregnant. Now that he has broken up with me and gone on to college I am still trying to get over that emotional connection. I am still dealing with a lot of hurt. I now know that I need to be in a relationship where I can have all the things I want emotionally without having the sex."
>
> HIGH SCHOOL GIRL

FREE VIDEO BONUS

Hear what a guy has to say about the 7 secrets.
Watch the videos NOW by going to:

www.7secretsofguys.com/videos

SECRET 5

They're not looking for a wife.

"My last girlfriend freaked me out because she always talked about what we would be doing in the future, as if we were going to get married. I decided to let her go because marriage was nowhere on my mind."

—High School Guy

PLAYER	GOOD GUY	BEST GUY
Not only is he not looking for a wife, he's not even faithful to his girlfriend.	Most guys aren't thinking about marrying you even though they are "committed" to you. Commitment does not equal marriage for him.	Loves his future wife even before he meets her. He's abstaining so he can give her the best of him and not the rest of him. Even so, it still doesn't mean he's looking for a wife.

"I texted my boyfriend during your class and told him I didn't want to have sex anymore. His reply was, 'Maybe we shouldn't be together.' He was three years older

than me, and I have known him all my life because he's a family friend. I actually thought we were gonna get married and we were in love."

※ HIGH SCHOOL GIRL

Girls are almost programmed at an early age to fantasize about weddings, marriages and the "happily ever after" dream. How many fairy tale movies are about a princess who gets rescued by a prince? These fairytale expectations lead many young ladies to convince themselves their boyfriends are just as focused on getting married as they are. And this is rarely the case.

A guy in one of my classes explained to me the difference between how girls and guys think about marriage. He said, "Girls wrap too much of their futures into marriage. And that's how they define success. To a teenage girl, getting married is one of her main goals. A teenage guy's first goal is to be successful. And after he's become successful, a wife becomes a part of his success. But marriage isn't how we define success, and definitely isn't our focus in high school like it is for girls."

I do think there is some truth in what he is saying when it comes to teenage girls. Although this doesn't apply to all girls, many tend to think about long-term relationships (a.k.a. marriage), long before guys do. You don't find television shows about weddings targeted to guys. Teen guys also haven't decided the style or color of tuxedo their groomsmen will wear in their weddings. Many teen girls can already describe the style of their wedding gown and tell you the color of their bridesmaids dresses.

I shared the comments from the young man above with a class of eighth-grade girls. One of the young ladies said, "Well, if guys don't plan to marry us, why would they date us?" I asked her if she thought every guy who dated a girl should be thinking of her as his future wife. She said, "I know sometimes things happen where it doesn't work out. But I think he should at least see her as a possibility. If not, he's just wasting her time." She vocalized what many young girls are thinking. But I doubt many eighth-grade boys have that same expectation. And if boys don't have the same expectations, then she's right: They're wasting each other's time.

This premature focus on marriage by teen girls is problematic. It causes girls to justify their decision to have sex because they're thinking, *we're going to get married anyway*.

Even when guys commit, how long do they expect the relationships to last?

Usually, guys are more realistic than girls when it comes to their expectations for the length of a relationship.

A young man once told me girls need to be able to handle the pain and the pleasure that come with a relationship. When I asked what he meant, he said, "Almost all teenage relationships are temporary, so girls need to enjoy the pleasure while you're together and expect the pain when it ends. Because, nine times out of ten, it's going to end. It's just a matter of time." If this is typical of guys' thoughts about relationships, it may explain why guys don't seem to be as devastated over a breakup as girls are.

Guys do tend to go into a relationship with the expectation it will end eventually.

> *If girls thought about the longevity of relationships more like the guys, they might be less heartbroken when relationships end.*

Girls often go into the relationship thinking it won't ever end. If girls thought about the longevity of relationships more like the guys, they might be less heartbroken when relationships end. It also may change what they're willing to do while in their relationships. The case study below provides a great example.

CASE STUDY
Chelsea and Kyle

I remember watching an episode of *The Oprah Winfrey Show* one day when Chelsea and Kyle, a fourteen-year-old couple, were on the show. They said they were ready to have sex. Their moms brought the couple to the show hoping Oprah and her guest therapist could talk the couple out of it.

Therapist: Chelsea and Kyle, how long do you plan to be together?

Chelsea and Kyle: A long time.

Therapist to Kyle: What does a long time mean to you?

Kyle: Six months to a year.

Chelsea gasps.

Kyle to Chelsea: What do you expect? We're still in high school.

Therapist to Chelsea: What did you have in mind when you said a long time?

Chelsea: Forever.

they're not looking for a wife

> *Chelsea had envisioned marrying Kyle, whereas Kyle saw the relationship as lasting no longer than a year.*
>
> **Therapist to Chelsea:** Would you have been so eager to have sex with Kyle had you known Kyle only expected to be with you for a year at most?
>
> **Chelsea:** No.

At first glance, Chelsea and Kyle seemed to be on the same page. After all, when asked how long they thought they would be together, they answered the question in unison, "a long time." Clearly their definitions were different.

What if Kyle and Chelsea's definitions of a long time were the same? Would it have been okay for them to have sex? My answer is still no. Even if they both believed they'd be together forever, they're only fourteen years old. Anything could happen within the next eight to ten years before marriage that could cause the relationship to end. His family or hers could move away, for example. As much as you may believe your life and circumstances will always be the way they are when you're a teenager, this is rarely the case.

Are you dating your future husband or just your future ex?

I was teaching a co-ed class of eighth-grade students and shared with them that girls tend to think about marriage long before boys do. I told them a girl is usually the one who sits in class and writes her first name with the boyfriend's last name. When

secret five

I said this, many of the students pointed to a young man in the class and laughed. I apologized to the young man and told him I wasn't aware many guys did this. He said, "I don't." The rest of the class said in unison, "But his girlfriend does." They said she drives them crazy because she sits in every class and writes her first name and his last name over and over.

I asked the young man, "Is the girl they're talking about your girlfriend? If so, do you plan to marry her?" He said "yes" and "no." As a matter of fact, his answer to whether he planned to marry her was a resounding "no." I asked him how he could be so sure he wouldn't marry his current girlfriend. He said, "Because when I go to high school next year, there will be girls I haven't even met yet." I would be willing to bet when this guy is a senior in high school, he'll say something similar if asked whether he plans to marry his girlfriend. "When I go to college next year, there will be girls in college I haven't even met yet."

It may sound cold for this guy to respond this way, but he makes a valid point. It would benefit girls to consider this point as well. At your age, why would you want to make a long-term commitment to someone right now when there are so many other guys out there you haven't even met?

Here's the reality: When you date someone, the relationship will likely end one of two ways—you will either marry him or break up with him. As a teenager, there's a much greater chance you'll break up than get married. This means most teenagers are dating their future ex.

> When you date someone, the relationship will likely end one of two ways—you will either marry him or break up with him.

"I think what got to me was when you said right now people date their future ex, unless it is who they will marry. So, I thought about it, and there really is no point in dating, at least not right now. I am more focused on my life, so I don't have time for someone else."

          HIGH SCHOOL GIRL

  Many girls I speak with come to the same conclusion as the young lady above. Based on the amount of drama and stress that comes with being in a temporary relationship, they just don't think the payout is worth it. They have figured out that their teen years won't last forever, and they would rather enjoy them with as little drama and stress as possible. Let's face it: even if sex isn't a part of a relationship, it will still require a lot of time and energy you could spend focusing on things that will be around long term, like friends, family, sports, hobbies, etc.

Does commitment equal marriage for guys?

Check out what a guy said in class one day, "Why is it girls think guys plan to marry them just because they're in a committed relationship or say they love them? Commitment doesn't mean forever or marriage. Just because I tell her I love her, it doesn't mean I plan to marry her. Why can't girls just enjoy being in a relationship without getting so uptight about how long it's going to last?"

  So if guys aren't thinking about marriage, what do they mean when they say they're in a committed relationship? When high school guys speak of commitment, most of them mean monogamous at best. Monogamous means they're loyal or devoted to a relationship with one person at a time,

secret five

but not necessarily forever. The *Player* might not even mean monogamous, but even the *Good Guy* and the *Best Guy* don't usually have marriage in mind when they date girls. Notice I didn't say "don't ever have marriage in mind." I'm sure there are teen guys who plan to marry the girls they date. They're just not the majority of guys.

Chapter 2 discussed some of the reasons guys may say they love you and not mean it. Let's be clear, even if they mean it when they say it, this still doesn't mean they plan to marry you.

> Good sex doesn't resolve conflict, pay bills or help you communicate.

And yet, many young women convince themselves they will marry the guys they date as teenagers. But, these same girls don't even know what qualities to look for in a potential spouse. When evaluating whether a guy is even future husband material, it's important to determine whether you both share the same values and goals for your future. You should also do things together that will show his character. Shared values, common goals and strong character are much more important in a potential life partnership than sex. This is why it's important to spend time getting to know a potential partner in ways that will benefit you more than just physically if you do marry.

Getting to know a potential partner beyond sex is also important because a lot of people let good sex convince them it's a good relationship. Then, when they get married, they realize they spend much more time out of the bed than they do in bed. Good sex doesn't resolve conflict, pay bills or help you communicate.

It's impossible to say no girl will ever marry her high school boyfriend. But it's also impossible to be one hundred percent confident a high school relationship will end in marriage. There's just no way to be sure. Only time will tell, but I do know the odds are against high school relationships leading to marriage. I've read statistics of anywhere from two percent to five percent of high school couples will get married and stay married.

Why can't guys commit—or can they?

Many girls just don't think guys can commit, but that's not true. Guys can and do commit. They commit all the time, when it's something they deem worth committing to—something they value and want in their lives for a long time. If you find a guy who wants to be a professional athlete, he'll get up at five a.m. to work out. A guy who wants to be a professional musician will spend hours practicing his instrument. Guys commit to things they value and think will be around for a long period of time. So if they're not committing to a relationship, it's most likely because they don't see it as something that will last forever.

A tenth-grade sexually active guy in one of my classes once explained why teenage boys don't commit in relationships. He said, "I don't understand why girls expect us to make a long-term commitment to them. We're too young and immature to commit. It's crazy for them to think we know who we want to be with forever when we don't even know ourselves. The person I'll be in five years is a different person than I am now." This boy understands he, and most of his peers, are still immature and don't know what they want in the future. Unfortunately, girls don't always understand this truth or the truth that they are still immature as well.

The question I have for girls is this: At your age, why do you want to make a commitment to someone who is immature and nine times out of ten won't be around a year or two from now?

secret five

Will sex make guys commit?

I've met three categories of girls who think sex will make a guy commit. In each of these situations, the answer to this question is *no*.

1 She's not dating him and knows he has no interest in dating her, but thinks sex will change his mind.

> *"The first day you came, I was planning to have sex with a guy I like a lot, but he just wanted sex from me. I knew this going into the relationship, but I still somehow thought I could change this by having sex with him."*
>
> — High School Girl

It's shocking that some girls think if a boy doesn't like them enough to commit, sex will somehow make him change his mind. This rarely works out. Once a girl tries to use her body to get attention or affection from a boy, she's already communicated to him she doesn't respect herself. Remember, if you don't respect yourself, he won't respect you, and he will never take you seriously as a girlfriend.

A *Player* may pretend to like a girl if it gets him sex, but as we've already covered, he only cares about what she's giving him. It's sad guys don't even have to pretend to like a girl nowadays to get sex. The following case study describes a situation in which a young lady wanted to date a guy who was her friend, and she thought having sex with him would change her status from friend to girlfriend.

CASE STUDY
Taylor and Zack

Taylor: I need to talk with you, but I don't want you to judge me after you hear what I have to say.

Me: *[I know I need to brace myself if she has to start the conversation with that disclaimer.]* Of course I won't judge you.

Taylor: My best friend's entire family is like my family, and I spend a lot of time at their house. I've always been close with my best friend's brother, Zack. I've had a crush on him for a long time and always wished we could be more than just friends. Here's the problem. He has a girlfriend. But she's a virgin and not planning to have sex with him. So, I thought since she's not putting out, maybe if I had sex with Zack he would leave his girlfriend and date me. So, I kept flirting with him, and one night we ended up having sex. It wasn't like we planned it that night, even though he knew I "liked him." We even kept having sex after that first time.

Me: Well, did you get what you wanted? Did he leave his girlfriend for you?

Taylor: No. Every time I asked him whether he was going to break up with her, he would say, "I can't, because she hasn't given me a reason to break up with her."

Me: Well, if he cared about you and wanted to be with you, the only reason he would need is that he found someone he likes better.

Taylor: The worse part is now he's avoiding me. Whenever I go to their house now, he either leaves or goes in his room and shuts the door. So, not only did he not become my boyfriend, I also lost him as a friend.

Me: I don't mean to sound harsh when I say what I'm about to say, but you need to know how Zack is processing what just happened. He knows you were willing to have sex with someone you weren't in a relationship with (him). In his mind, if you'll have sex with him without a commitment, he can only believe you would have sex with someone else you're not in a relationship with too. That's not attractive to a guy.

Taylor starts crying.

Me: Would you still date Zack if he were to come to you tomorrow and ask you to be his girlfriend?

Taylor: Yes.

Me: Why would you want to date someone with his character? He cheated on his girlfriend with you, so what does that make him?

Taylor (reluctantly): A cheater.

Me: Do you want to be in a relationship with a cheater?

they're not looking for a wife

Young ladies often believe sex will change their relationship status from friend to girlfriend. But guys don't think this way. As a result, instead of sex making Zack fall in love with Taylor, sex made the relationship awkward. Zack only wanted to have fun, but now realizes Taylor wanted more than that. He isn't willing or able to give her what she expects, so he begins to avoid her, and she's hurt and confused by what just happened.

2   She is dating him and believes if she has sex with him, he'll stay with her longer.

> *"My boyfriend has been wanting us to have sex for quite some time now, and I always agreed for fear he would leave me if I didn't."*
>
> — HIGH SCHOOL GIRL

This girl had sex with her boyfriend just because she feared he would leave. A *Player* may even threaten to leave if sex doesn't happen. But in either case, why would a girl want to be with a guy who won't stay with her if she's not having sex? If a guy is willing to leave because you won't have sex, that means he values the sex more than he values you. This should be a deal breaker. This is why I'm shocked that girls use sex to try to keep a guy who's already revealing his true colors. But it's common.

> *If a guy is willing to leave because you won't have sex, that means he values the sex more than he values you.*

Even though some *Players* use the threat of leaving to get sex, it surprises a lot of guys that girls will use sex to try to keep a guy around.

secret five

> "I went back to ask my ex-girlfriend if she regretted any of the times we had sex. She said she did and she would sometimes have sex with me so she wouldn't lose me. After hearing that from her, I felt like crap."
>
> ～ HIGH SCHOOL GUY

{ **74%** (three out of four) of guys say sex wouldn't make them stay in a relationship they didn't want to be in. }

Notice she's his ex-girlfriend, which means the sex she used to keep him didn't make him stay. Instead of keeping her boyfriend, she was only left with regrets.

Young ladies, real love is unconditional. You don't have to do or give anything to get it. If having sex with him is a requirement for him to be with you, he doesn't love you. He loves what he's getting from you. If he loved you, you wouldn't have to give him anything for him to stay.

A lot of young women will have sex with their boyfriends just because all of his other girlfriends had sex with him. They think they have to do the same to keep him. If sex wasn't enough for him to stay with his previous girlfriends, it probably won't make him stay this time either. This is just another example of young ladies mistakenly thinking sex is the key to maintaining a relationship.

3 **He broke up with her, but she thinks if she keeps having sex with him, he'll start dating her again.**

> "I've been in 'love' with my ex-boyfriend since we ended things. Although the relationship ended, we continued

to have sex. My young mind thought if I kept putting out, he'd come back. After listening to you speak, I realized I'm hurting no one but myself. I have never felt so worthless in my life 'til the day I found out he was dating another girl and taking her to prom. I did nothing but cry."

—High School Girl

> *If having sex with him is a requirement for him to be with you, he doesn't love you.*

This is, unfortunately, an incredibly common story. It makes sense that a girl may still have feelings for her boyfriend even after the relationship ends. But it doesn't make sense to use sex to get him back. Even if it works, he's coming back for the sex, not you.

There's also a second reason girls will continue having sex with ex-boyfriends: They believe based on their sexual history, it's safer to continue having sex with the ex-boyfriend than risk getting an STD from a new partner. Here's the problem with that logic: if he's not dating her anymore, then he's no longer committed to a monogamous relationship with her. Therefore, it's likely he's also having sex with someone besides her. This new partner could infect him with an STD, putting her at risk of contracting one as well.

How can sex with a future ex complicate your life?

When I ask students in my classes how many have dated someone they knew they didn't want to marry, most of the students will raise their hands. When it comes to dating, there's nothing wrong with dating someone you don't intend to marry if sex isn't a part of the relationship. You're just screening potential candidates to understand what you may or may not like in a future partner. This process only becomes a problem when you have sex, like the young man below describes:

> "If you want to prevent guys like me from having sex, you should ask them how they feel about the girl they're with. Because I liked the girl [I was having sex with], but not enough to spend the rest of my life with her if I got her pregnant. I can take responsibility for my child. But when you have a child with someone you are stuck with her and all the drama that's attached to her. Even if you don't get married or if you move 100,000 miles away from her, your child will keep you tied together for life. That alone scares me to death, not to mention all the other possible outcomes that could have happened."
>
> ~ HIGH SCHOOL GUY

What normally happens when a guy who isn't thinking about marriage gets a girl pregnant? Too often the guy just leaves. Even if it's a *Good Guy* who stays for the child's sake, it creates a lot of difficulty for him and the mother if they didn't plan on staying together. They're now linked by a whole new life for eighteen-plus years.

> "Life has been so hard since the day my daughter was born . . . I wish I could have waited for Mrs. Right because my girlfriend loves me, but I don't feel the same way about her anymore, and I don't even know how to deal with that. I will stick it out though because the only memory that plays in my head is [that] my father wasn't

there. My story is full of regret where a few minutes of pleasure turned into eighteen-plus years of hardship."

~High School Guy

Wouldn't you rather be with someone who wants to be in a relationship with you instead of someone who is only "sticking it out" because he got you pregnant? This isn't even the worst-case scenario in which the father walks away entirely. But still, no one wins—not the mother, the father, or the child being raised by parents who don't love each other.

Why do guys look for different qualities in wives than girlfriends?

Although teen guys may not be looking for wives right now, that doesn't mean they don't know what qualities they want their future wives to have. Even though most guys have an idea of what they want in a wife, they may still date someone who doesn't have those qualities. They don't expect her to be their wife anyway. The standards they have for Mrs. Right are often different than they are for Ms. Right Now.

In the past, I've conducted a revealing activity with groups of guys. I asked them to list the qualities they desire when looking for a girlfriend. Then I asked them to list the qualities they would desire when they begin looking for a wife.

Most times, the guys had different things on each list. The qualities on the girlfriend list focused more on superficial or physical characteristics like pretty, nice figure, big boobs and big butt. The qualities on the wife list focused on more substantial things like honest, loyal, intelligent, ambitious and emotionally stable. The difference in standards makes sense when you think

secret five

about the fact they consider girlfriends temporary and wives permanent.

Teen guys may already know what qualities they want in a wife. But, marriage is so far in the future for them they don't feel it's necessary to even consider those standards in a girlfriend.

A young man in one of my classes told me he was dating a girl who had "daddy issues." He complained about how difficult it was to be in a relationship with her as a result of those issues. I spoke with him after class, and during our conversation, he told me they were sexually active. I asked him if he planned to marry her. He rolled his eyes and said, "No way. She has too many issues." And yet, he was dating her and having sex with her. I wondered whether she had any clue the guy she was dating and having sex with was already sure she wasn't wife material. She met his standards for a girlfriend, but she didn't meet his standards for a wife. She may not have had any idea he saw her that way.

I definitely don't condone this young man's behavior. But let me share an analogy that may explain why he thinks and behaves the way he does. Would you have higher standards for a car you were renting or a car you were purchasing? You'd most likely have higher standards for the purchased vehicle because the rental car is only temporary. If anything is wrong with it or happens to it, you can just return it and get another one. The quality of the car just wouldn't be as important.

If you buy a car, would you prefer a new car or a pre-owned car? You'd probably prefer a new car if you could afford it. If you couldn't afford a new car, would you prefer a car with 10,000,

> *...marriage is so far in the future for them they don't feel it's necessary to even consider those standards in a girlfriend.*

30,000 or 80,000 miles on it? You'd probably prefer the car with 10,000 miles because the higher the mileage, the greater the chance it'll have issues. It may need new tires, timing belt, transmission, brakes, etc.

I'm sure you have figured out by now the rental car represents the girlfriend and the purchased car represents the wife in this analogy (To be clear: I'm in no way implying a girlfriend/wife is considered a man's property. I'm simply using this analogy to prove a point about temporary versus long-term value).

Just as a person would have higher standards for the car they purchased than the car they rented, the standards used by most guys when selecting their wives are typically higher than those used when selecting their girlfriends. We've already established why. They have no intention of being with their girlfriends long term.

> …most high school guys tell me they would love to marry a virgin. They know she won't give them any STDs.

Let's talk about one of the standards some guys have for their future wives. Just as most guys tell me they would rather buy a brand-new car, most high school guys tell me they would love to marry a virgin. They know she won't give them any STDs. They won't have to worry about dealing with another man if she had a child. And they won't have to deal with any emotional consequences she may have suffered. Just like the more miles a car has on it, the greater the chance something may be wrong with it, guys believe the more sexual partners a girl has, the greater the chance she will bring baggage into a marriage. This is why many guys would prefer a virgin bride.

Some guys will also have different standards for themselves than they do for their future wives, which clearly isn't fair.

> *"I was surprised by the wake-up call that I harbored a double standard. I intended to marry a girl who was a virgin, who had saved herself just for marriage, but I personally did not plan to use any self-control when it comes to sex before marriage."*
>
> ~ H<small>IGH</small> S<small>CHOOL</small> G<small>UY</small>

If this young man's goal was to marry a virgin and he's having sex with girls he isn't married to, wouldn't that disqualify the girls he's dating as candidates to be his wife? This young man is not alone. Many young men will have sex with their girlfriends, disqualifying them from becoming their wives. Furthermore, these young men will have as much sex as they want without any thought about the baggage they could bring into a marriage (i.e., the potential drama from a relationship with the mother of his child or an STD), but hold girls and potential wives to a much higher behavioral standard. This isn't fair and it isn't right, but it's something of which all girls should be aware.

Now that you know . . .

I understand there is a lot of pressure placed on teens to be in a relationship. I can't tell you whether a relationship is right for you right now. I will tell you not to buckle to the pressure from the media, society and/or your peers that makes girls feel like they are undesirable or less valuable if they aren't in a relationship. A relationship should not define you.

Guys know most teenage relationships are short term, and they're not looking for anything more. Knowing a relationship will most likely end should affect your behavior within it.

they're not looking for a wife

Don't risk your long-term physical and emotional health for a relationship that's most likely short term.

> "You helped me realize I'm proud to have a girlfriend that says no to sex because it helps me realize what I want in a woman. I don't want a girl that's willing to give up sex within a year, or even before marriage. I want a girl with values, one who wants me for who I am, and I want her for who she is and why she's special."
>
> ~ HIGH SCHOOL GUY

A relationship should not define you.

Your teen years shouldn't be about compromising for short-term relationships. Instead, spend them discovering all the wonderful things about you that make you the special and unique person you are.

Just as teenage guys aren't looking for a wife, teenage girls shouldn't waste time looking to be one. Guys aren't and shouldn't be any teen girl's priority.

SECRET 6

They can't replace your father.

"I don't have a father in my life, so when you spoke about girls looking for a lot of things in guys to fill the void in their hearts their fathers left, I could relate to that. I see that in myself every day. But I'm learning to love myself more than any man ever loved me and to find my full potential and self-worth."

— High School Girl

PLAYER	GOOD GUY	BEST GUY
Specifically goes after the girl with daddy issues and takes advantage of her vulnerability.	May or may not recognize daddy issues are connected to her decision to have sex.	Is a protector and not a predator; will never take advantage of a girl who has daddy issues.

This is a particularly difficult topic to discuss because every situation is unique. I often feel inadequate when trying to counsel girls dealing with pain resulting from an issue as complicated as fatherlessness. The ideal solution would be for all fathers to understand the importance of their presence in the lives of their children. Short of that, I can only help girls develop healthy coping mechanisms to address the emotional consequences.

> *Many young women [are] ... actually trying to fill the void left by an absent or disengaged father.*

In a perfect world, every daughter would have a great father who validates, protects, guides and provides for her. As a little girl, her father would be there to hug and kiss her, tuck her in at night, surprise her with unexpected gifts and teach her how to ride her tricycle. These simple interactions send a powerful message to a young girl that she's valuable, safe, cared for and loved. Being secure in these areas early on allows little girls to grow into secure, confident and accomplished young ladies.

Without a father around to do these things, far too many girls grow up with low self-esteem, a lack of confidence and a fear of rejection. These negative emotions can have a huge impact on a young woman's sense of self, which often translates into poor relationship choices.

> "Reflecting on my daddy issues makes me realize the causes of some of the bad choices I've made in the past with other guys are due to a lack of trust, fear of being ignored and fear of being hurt. I don't know what to do because every issue I have with my father somehow affects my relationships."
>
> HIGH SCHOOL GIRL

Many young women find themselves in a downward spiral of poor sexual decisions, only to realize they're actually trying to fill the void left by an absent or disengaged father. These girls mistakenly believe a relationship will make up for all the love and validation they didn't get from their fathers.

> "My dad doesn't care about me. I have had sex with my boyfriend once, and I did it because I wanted to feel loved. My boyfriend told me he couldn't replace the things my dad didn't do for me, all he can do is help me through it. We have stopped having sex and are now focused on the future."
>
> —High School Girl

A lot of young men can sense when young ladies are dealing with issues resulting from an absent or emotionally disengaged father. They say these girls are often needy and have higher expectations from them than girls who have good relationships with their fathers.

> "When you talked about girls and daddy issues, I thought about my ex-girlfriend. Her father abandoned her at a young age, and she hates her stepfather. I liked her, but she was jealous and had high expectations of me. After we broke up, I realized she wanted me to fill a position I couldn't fill—the love of a father. You confirmed it when you came to speak to us."
>
> —High School Guy

It's important for girls to acknowledge that a void exists so they can stop looking to guys to fill it. *Players* will purposely use a young lady's pain to their advantage. They'll give her temporary attention to get sex without caring about the impact it will have on her. *Good Guys* may also end up having sex with girls who have daddy issues even if they didn't set out to take advantage of them. *Best Guys* will help girls understand sex will never fill the void of a missing father.

The benefits of an actively engaged father:

Young ladies who've never had a father in their lives or homes may not even know what they're missing. When they don't recognize the benefits of having an actively engaged father, it becomes difficult to recognize their poor choices may be related to his absence. If you didn't have a father figure in your life, it's important to understand the benefits of a father's presence to prevent his absence from affecting your decision-making. The following are a few benefits of a father's presence:

> *If your father isn't in your life and you recognize your self-worth is lacking, you will have to develop it yourself.*

A father validates.

Fathers should be the first man to make a little girl feel loved, to tell her she's beautiful and to show her how much she's worth. A real father also encourages his daughter's talents and supports and celebrates her achievements. This is crucial in building a young girl's self-esteem and confidence in her own worth. When a father does this, she doesn't need any other guy down the road to validate her—her father's already done that.

If your father isn't in your life and you recognize your self-worth is lacking, you will have to develop it yourself. You should spend the necessary time discovering what you excel in and what makes you special. This self-discovery is the first step toward building your self-confidence and sense of value.

A father shares his strategy.

When I asked a father once how he planned to educate his seven-year-old daughter about relationships, guys, sex, etc., he asked me a question "Do you know how banks train their tellers to recognize counterfeit money?" He said, "They actually make them study genuine/real money. They become so familiar with real money that the counterfeit money is easy to detect." Likewise, he spends a great deal of time with his daughter showing her what real love looks like so she won't accept anything less from any guy she dates. Real love is unconditional and requires nothing in return.

> *A father models... how men and women should treat each other in a relationship.*

A father provides.

When the subject of a father providing for his daughter comes up, people normally think about financial support. But, there's so much more a father provides for a daughter. A father models with his spouse (and/or her mother) how men and women should treat each other in a relationship. He also sets the bar for the type of relationships she should have with guys when she matures. If a father does this well, his daughter learns how to set the bar for the type and caliber of boyfriend she chooses and how she should be treated.

If you don't have a positive relationship with an actively engaged father, you should ask your parent/guardian for help in identifying positive adult male role models to serve as your example.

I watched a documentary on fatherlessness once. The "expert" was a high school principal of a school with a large percentage of students whose fathers weren't in their homes. The principal shared a story about one of his fatherless female students he felt was longing for a father's guidance. This young lady was dating a guy the principal thought wasn't the caliber of guy she should be dating. He was quick to tell her she deserved someone who was more focused on his education and success. He noticed how she glowed when hearing a father figure put her on a pedestal and tell her a guy wasn't good enough for her. Imagine how differently young ladies' relationship choices would be if their fathers only confirmed for them what they deserved.

> *Young men ... often try to have sex with girls from single-parent homes more quickly than they will try for girls who have fathers in their lives.*

A father protects.

A father usually protects the home and keeps his family safe, but his protection isn't just physical—he also protects his daughter from boyfriends who may not have her best interests at heart. A great father will have a conversation with any and every guy his daughter dates to share his expectations for how they will treat his daughter. This conversation, or often even the father's mere presence can ensure every guy his daughter dates will treat her with the utmost respect.

If you don't have a father in your life, you should be aware of the tactics some guys use to take advantage of the fact that your father isn't present so you don't fall for them.

Young men have told me they often try to have sex with girls from single-parent homes more quickly than they will try for girls who have fathers in their lives. They do this out of fear and respect for the father. They're afraid of what a father will do if he finds out they're having sex with his daughter. They also respect him because they know he was just like them once, and he knows exactly what they're thinking. They say it's much easier to win over and/or fool a mother. The problem with that logic, of course, is girls with single mothers are already statistically at greater risk for becoming single mothers themselves. Also, if these young men get one of those young women pregnant without any intention of being with her long term, their future daughters will likely be raised in the same single-parent household they preyed on. This puts their daughters in a vulnerable position, and the cycle continues.

Not every guy makes a calculated decision to target girls from single-parent homes. There are plenty of teenage girls from two-parent homes getting pressured for sex as well. But all young ladies need to be aware that some guys do make decisions to date a girl based on how easily they think it'll be to have sex. Fatherlessness is just one factor they consider.

A father guides.

Fathers provide their daughters with guidance in many important areas—including navigating relationships with the opposite sex. Because fathers were once teenage boys, they can tell their daughters exactly what the average teenage boy is thinking. A father who provides his daughter with a male perspective helps his daughter figure out how to form nonsexual relationships with guys. When a father does a good job of informing his daughter, she already knows the secrets in this book. She also understands sex should never be a requirement in a relationship.

If you don't have a father in your life, you should seek guidance from older brothers, trustworthy male friends and/or other male relatives to get the inside scoop on how guys think.

> "When I got to high school, my older brother was twenty-three at the time. He realized he didn't want me treating sex casually, so he changed the way he approached women and became abstinent and talked to me about not having sex or doing sexual things in a relationship just to please your partner or keep him. I have three older brothers who set an amazing example for me."
>
> —HIGH SCHOOL GIRL

The most common consequences of fatherlessness:

Although all four of the above benefits are important, validation tends to have the most bearing on sexual decisions. When young women don't get unconditional love, attention and validation from their fathers, they often end up seeking it from any male and will give anything—including their bodies—to get it.

they can't replace your father

> "I'm that girl that has had 'daddy issues,' and even though it's hard to admit, I've realized that I have sought out validation in boys."
>
> — HIGH SCHOOL GIRL

A lack of validation often results in a pattern of poor choices I've seen fall into two categories:

1 **Self-medication:** Young women who fall into this pattern often try to medicate the pain of fatherlessness. They may become sexually active early on, engage with many sexual partners, abuse alcohol and other drugs and/or self-harm.

2 **Fear of rejection:** Young women who fall into this pattern will emotionally cling to guys who don't have their best interests at heart, have a difficult time letting go of harmful relationships, struggle to trust guys, and/or overachieve to prove they shouldn't have been rejected.

Though they result in varying issues, both of these behavioral patterns stem from a need for validation that a father figure should have provided.

> "I am sexually active, and this girl is the perfect example of what you spoke about. I have noticed she has low self-esteem because of how jealous she is. She uses sex to feel the love she lacked in her broken home, and she says I'm 'everything' to her. She keeps me around so she can hear she's beautiful. She's broken inside and out."

> *Normally a guy takes advantage of a girl like this, but I don't want to fit the stereotype of the typical guy. But if we don't have sex, it rips her apart inside. She assumes the worst and feels if we're not having sex, she's either unattractive or I'm cheating on her. What is the best way to go about fixing this? I don't want to have sex, but she doesn't understand."*
>
> ~ HIGH SCHOOL GUY

I would tell this young man, just as I would tell any young lady in a similar situation, any time you're doing something you don't want to do, that's not healthy. My advice to him would be to end the relationship. His girlfriend has some serious self-esteem issues that no amount of sex with him will fix. The longer he stays in the relationship and continues to have sex, the worse it will get.

The problem for girls who are lacking the validation from their fathers is twofold. First, some might feel they don't deserve real love if their fathers didn't love them. These girls think if their fathers didn't value or want them, then they must not be worth much at all. If a person doesn't think she's worth anything, she may be willing to give herself up for anything. In these unfortunate cases, a guy doesn't even have to say he loves her, tell her she's beautiful, or commit to dating her to get sex. She doesn't think she deserves these things anyway. How heartbreaking!

> *"What you said about girls with daddy issues hit close to home. Growing up, my father was an alcoholic. He wasn't around much at all. Here I was thinking, 'How much worth does a girl have with a nonexistent father?'*

Your speaking influenced me to realize my worth. I am worth something."

— High School Girl

The second problem many girls without fathers in their lives may face is a craving for the love and attention they never got.

"I've had tough times with my dad my whole life. I've always sought love in guys to help compensate for that lack of love and confidence. Now that I know I'm not alone and it's a common way of coping, I've stopped."

— High School Girl

They mistake a boy's attention for a man who actually cares, and they're willing to do whatever it takes to keep the attention coming. In these cases, these young girls end up putting their health and futures in jeopardy for a little attention that is most often fleeting. And they still can't replace the love they're actually searching for.

"I'm seventeen, and in the second semester of my freshman year alone I had nineteen sexual partners. I'm lucky enough to not have a child, but I do have HPV. I have no idea who gave it to me, and I don't know who I've infected. Now I'm a senior and I've had twenty-three sexual partners. No, I didn't have my father in my life, and until you spoke, I had no idea it had such an impact. It does make sense. Also, I have horrible self-esteem, and I'm looking to boys for love and affection. When you

spoke, you made me realize I am worth something and I don't need to do this to get love. Thank you so much for helping me realize this."

— HIGH SCHOOL GIRL

> *Using sex to heal abandonment issues is like using acid to heal an open wound. It only makes the problem worse.*

Promiscuity in particular is extremely detrimental behavior many girls fall victim to. When young ladies tell me they medicate their pain with sex, I ask, "How is that working for you?" They usually acknowledge it isn't working at all. I tell them that's because they are using the wrong medicine to fix the problem. Using sex to heal abandonment issues is like using acid to heal an open wound. It only makes the problem worse. Unfortunately, many girls don't realize this until it's too late. When the media manipulates young girls into believing sex equals love, it seems logical to heal the pain of abandonment with sex. It may seem logical, but it doesn't work.

If you identify with any of the above poor choices and don't have an active relationship with your father, please know your healing won't come from sex. Even if a guy wanted to take on the challenge of providing all the things a girl's father didn't, he couldn't. Why? Even with all his good intentions, as a teen, he's just not equipped to meet such a tall order. Providing for someone else's emotional needs is a lot to ask when he's still trying to figure out his own life. Bottom line: He's just a child himself, no matter how mature he appears to be. He shouldn't be burdened with the extra responsibility of establishing a girl's confidence and self-worth.

they can't replace your father

Often when I attribute girls' sexual decisions to pain from an absent father, there are girls in class who are offended. If they don't react visibly in class, they'll send me an angry letter later telling me the absence of their fathers hasn't driven them into the beds of guys. I'm afraid these girls may feel my statement implies they're lacking or less than, and that's definitely not my intent because it's not true. I will never say every girl without a father will make poor relationship and/or sexual decisions as a result. But I do have enough data/letters to confidently state many young ladies do, because they're trying to fill their "daddy void" with relationships.

So what's a girl to do?

If this were a fairytale, I would wave my magic wand so all girls would have a healthy relationship with their fathers. Maybe then they wouldn't feel the need to substitute sex for the love they seek from their dads. But this isn't a fairytale, and I don't have any magical powers. What I can do is offer some tips that may be useful on the journey toward healing, no matter what your current relationship is with your father.

Enlist the help of your mom. Even if your parents don't have a good relationship with each other, that doesn't mean you can't work on building one with your dad. Consider having an honest conversation with your mom about the impact your dad's absence has on you. See if she'd be willing to reach out to your father on your behalf and help clear a path toward reconciliation between you two. If she's not open to that, keep in mind there may be a lot of history between your parents you don't know about. Maybe all you get at first is honest dialogue about both of your feelings on the subject. And that's okay, because lasting change doesn't happen overnight. So be patient and keep your expectations realistic.

I recognize this might be easier said than done for some of you because your dad may have passed away, or you don't even know who he is. And still others of you have a dad who, for whatever reason, doesn't value the position he should have in your life. If that's the case, I want to encourage you that you're not alone and you can still lead a productive life.

Discover what makes you special. What do you enjoy doing? What are you gifted in? What's your passion? Focus on nurturing that. Even if you don't feel your father recognized it, you can recognize it in yourself.

That's not to say once you figure out what you want to do with your life, all your issues with your dad will magically disappear. But, having a vision and pursuing your purpose have a way of spilling over into those deep, empty spaces in your life like no boy ever could.

Address the pain. You may be thinking it doesn't matter that your father is not present. Many times, we repress our pain to avoid confronting the sadness. Or, you may not even recognize what you are feeling is pain because it feels more like anger. What you must understand is you have to deal with the pain head-on to get healing and avoid a lifetime of bad choices. That may sound impossible, but here are a few steps you can take:

> *...having a vision and pursuing your purpose have a way of spilling over into those deep, empty spaces in your life like no boy ever could.*

1 **Journal your feelings or thoughts.** Getting your emotions out on paper can be a great way to help you understand yourself better and trace your actions to the feelings that may be causing them.

2 **Write a letter to your father whether you send it or not.** I would encourage you to share this with him so you know he's aware of your feelings. The goal is not to bash him, but to make him aware of the pain you feel as a result of him not being there for you as a dedicated father. Again, if your father is no longer living, or you have no idea who he is and/or where he lives, the act of writing your feelings down on paper is still powerful. Write the letter anyway and shred it afterward. In your case, the objective is to do a pain dump and begin to release those feelings of hurt and abandonment.

> *Choosing not to forgive is like holding onto a hot coal and expecting it to burn the other person and not you.*

You should also try to forgive your father for his lack of involvement. You may not feel like he deserves it, but the forgiveness isn't for him—it's for you. Choosing not to forgive is like holding onto a hot coal and expecting it to burn the other person and not you. Focus only on how you feel—healing is for you and no one else.

> "I now know I need to stop looking for love in all the wrong places and to let go of all the pain and hurt from my father."
>
> — HIGH SCHOOL GIRL

3 **If nothing else helps, consider professional counseling.** You shouldn't have to heal alone. Help for you may best come in the form of counseling from a licensed counselor. Ask your mom about researching local options (Tip: Check with your local United Way for low-cost and/or free resources.). If professional counseling is not an option, seek the help of your mother, a grandparent, a school counselor or your faith leader. The goal is to rid yourself of all negative and non-productive emotions so you can heal and lead a happy, healthy life.

No matter the outcome, know that you are and always have been worthy of a father's love.

Now that you know . . .

If this chapter applies to you, you now know how the absence of a father can affect how guys approach you and how you see yourself. With that in mind, remember a guy can never make up for what your father didn't provide. If you're sexually active, ask yourself whether the temporary attention is benefiting your long-term healing or just putting your future child at risk of being in the same situation.

Now that you know better, you can do better. You deserve to feel great about yourself, and with the right steps, healing is possible.

> "Hearing you speak made me want to be more passionate about changing how I am. No more running to a boy expecting him to do my father's job."
>
> — High School Girl

SECRET 7

They will wait if you will.

"When you came, it made me think back to freshman year when my girlfriend and I were alone at her house. We were watching a movie and, all of a sudden she started touching me... I told her I wasn't ready for that step in the relationship. We had been going out for six months. I told her I wanted to wait but she didn't, so she broke up with me. At first I questioned why I said no. In my mind I wanted to, but my heart told me it wasn't worth it because I was not in love with her and I didn't want to hurt her. After you talked to us, I was so grateful for resisting that night. I didn't lose something good, but she did."

~High School Guy

PLAYER	GOOD GUY	BEST GUY
Won't wait—or at least not for long.	Will wait if you will.	Will wait even if you won't.

secret seven

This chapter addresses what I think is the most surprising of the seven secrets. It was important for me to end with this one because I want to give you hope that it's possible to find a guy who will love and respect you enough to wait.

> "I bet you don't receive many letters from a guy who actually is in search of a relationship without sex, but I am. I just wish a girl would know a kind, respectful man when she saw one."
>
> ~ HIGH SCHOOL GUY

I get a lot of letters like this one above. But girls don't believe it, so I try to share them as often as possible. Every time I do, girls are surprised. A lot of girls think, *even if we want to wait to have sex, we'll never find a guy who is willing to wait.* This isn't true. I've met plenty of guys who don't want sex from their girlfriends.

Do you remember the three types of guys I've been discussing in each chapter—the *Player*, the *Good Guy* and the *Best Guy*? Of course the *Player* won't be willing to wait, but the other two types of guys are willing to wait:

1. The *Best Guy*—He's abstaining, even at the risk of losing his girlfriend.
2. The *Good Guy*—He may be having sex, but would abstain if:
    a. he didn't think his girlfriend expected sex, and/or
    b. he was educated on how true love is shown.

Let's talk about the first type of guy, The *Best Guy*.

> "I want you to know I discussed with my girlfriend that I would like to wait until marriage, and then she left me. But that's okay. I am keeping my virginity as long as I can, up until marriage. I am a star on the basketball team, and it's hard to have self-control with all these females coming after me."
>
> ~ HIGH SCHOOL GUY

Often, girls think the *Best Guys* who are virgins or are saving themselves for marriage must be nerds, boring or lame. But this guy was the star of the basketball team and likely got more attention than the average nice guy. And even if he wasn't a star athlete, he'd still be a great guy. It's a shame many young ladies miss out on their *Best Guy* because he doesn't fit the image of their ideal guy.

The second group, the *Good Guys*, can fall in one of two categories. The first category includes the guys who don't necessarily want to have sex. They're only asking girls to have sex because that's what's expected of them.

> "I've had sex before. After your class, I told him I was done with sex. I'm thankful he respected my decision. Not only did he understand, but he also agreed. He said he was too afraid to come out and say it himself because of what I might have thought."
>
> ~ HIGH SCHOOL GIRL

The second category includes the guys who genuinely care for their girlfriends. They just haven't thought about how love is best shown. Once these guys understand, they're more than willing to stop having sex.

> *"You have helped me tell my girlfriend we should stop having sex because like you said, 'If you love someone, you won't risk their future.' I have told my girlfriend no to sex so I won't ruin our futures."*
>
> ~High School Guy

False assumptions girls make about guys:

Let's talk about three of the biggest assumptions I've heard girls make about guys.

1. Every guy wants sex.
2. If a guy doesn't want sex, something is wrong.
3. Giving a guy something is better than nothing.

Assumption 1: Every guy wants sex.

> *"I'm currently in love with one amazing girl, and I know I'm in love because I would do anything for her, and I would die trying to protect her. I don't need sex from her to have a good relationship, and she feels the exact same way."*
>
> ~High School Guy

Take a look at the survey data on the opposite page. This means over half of teen boys do not want sex. Unfortunately, girls often assume they have to offer or agree to sex if they expect to have or keep a boyfriend. The truth is not every boy wants sex. According to the survey data, more than fifty percent of

they will wait if you will

guys want to get to know you for you. Yet, girls keep making decisions based on what the smaller, maybe more vocal percentage of guys wants. Some of the guys included in this fifty-six percent may have even asked their girlfriends for sex. But what you don't know is they were hoping those girlfriends would say no.

> **56%**—More than half of the young men surveyed said they were relieved when their girlfriends wanted to wait to have sex.

Here's an example of what happens all too often:

A young man doesn't want to have sex. Deep down in his heart, sex goes against his values and comes with consequences he'd rather not face. But he thinks everyone expects him to have sex, even his girlfriend. So he asks her for sex, hoping and praying she'll say no. The young lady who wrote the letter below was dating one of those guys.

> *"I could relate when you said some guys are only asking for sex because they are afraid of what the girl will think if they don't ask. My boyfriend asked me if I wanted to have sex. When I told him I wanted to wait until I got married, he started smiling from ear to ear. He said he was happy that I wanted to wait because he was afraid he'd never find a girl who shared his values."*
>
> — HIGH SCHOOL GIRL

On the other side of this scenario, you have a young lady who also doesn't want to have sex. Deep down in her heart, she also knows sex comes with consequences she doesn't want to face or goes against her values. But she thinks if she doesn't have sex with her boyfriend she may lose him. So she agrees to have sex with him. Check out the letter below from a guy who dated a girl like this:

> "Your talk made me go talk to my girlfriend who I have been dating since ninth grade. I am now a senior, and I told her I wanted to stop having sex. She was my first, and I was hers. She understood where I was coming from and told me she was only having sex with me because she thought I wanted it. We are still dating, but we are no longer sexually active."
>
> ~High School Guy

As a result of the false assumptions, two people are making what could have been a life-altering decision to do something neither of them wanted to do. They only made the decision because it was what they thought they were supposed to do or what they assumed the other person wanted. How crazy is that? If they hadn't stopped having sex, they both could have ended up resenting each other for making them do something they didn't want to do.

But smart people make poor choices every day, especially when it comes to sex.

Let's see how this scenario played out with a sexually active college student I spoke with.

She told me she hated how she felt after having sex with her boyfriend and would take a million showers afterward. Sex brought back memories of her uncle raping her when she was younger. When I offered to talk with her boyfriend, she begged me not to do so because it wasn't his fault

they will wait if you will

she was having sex. She was the one who initiated the sex. I told her I didn't understand why she would initiate sex when it had such a negative effect on her. She said, "Because all guys want sex, and I wanted to make him happy."

This girl is prioritizing a guy's happiness over what she believes is best for her. I'm sure she's a smart girl, yet she is making such an "unsmart" decision. But smart people make poor choices every day, especially when it comes to sex.

Everyone would be so much better off if young men and young ladies only made decisions they wanted to make and felt good about. Instead, many are making decisions they assume they have to make to please their girlfriend/boyfriend, to fit in or to be popular.

When I share the above story in class, I ask the guys whether all guys want sex. The answer is always a resounding no, which surprises many of the girls in class. Many of the guys are just as surprised girls would even assume they do.

Assumption 2: If he doesn't want sex, there's something wrong.

A lot of guys feel stuck between a rock and a hard place. If they don't try to have sex with their girlfriends, one of three things will happen:

1. Their girlfriends will think they're gay.

   > "My boyfriend and I have been together for a year now, and he has never talked about having sex until I brought it to his attention recently. Like you said, some girls think they have gay men if they don't talk about and ask for sex. That is what I thought."
   >
   > — HIGH SCHOOL GIRL

2. Their girlfriends will think they don't find them attractive.

> "I actually like this girl, and she asked me to have sex, and I only knew her for a month and a half. But when I said no, she thought something was wrong with her, when it was just that I didn't want anything bad to happen."
>
> ~HIGH SCHOOL GUY

3. Their girlfriends will think they're cheating on them.

> "After school on Friday, me and my girlfriend were about to have sex, and I said to her, 'We don't have to do this if you don't want to. I don't want you to think I'm using you because I'm not. I can go on till marriage without this.' She was furious. She got up and began to question if I was cheating on her. She started asking me if I was getting it from some other girl and if I didn't want her anymore. I sat her down and told her where I was coming from, but . . . she still either wants to have sex with me or thinks I must be cheating."
>
> ~HIGH SCHOOL GUY

Unfortunately, girls have a hard time believing a guy who doesn't ask for sex is doing so just because he loves the girl too much to jeopardize her future.

This is a tough position for a guy to be in, especially when he also has societal pressures telling him sex is what makes him a man. This is bad enough by itself, but now he's getting more pressure from the girl he likes when he's just trying to do the right thing.

Many girls have told me they understood the girlfriend's suspicions. They admitted they would also wonder whether he was cheating. Is this something you might think as well?

Girls say they want a guy who wants them for who they are and not for sex. Yet, at the same time, if a guy doesn't ask for sex, girls begin to question his masculinity, her attractiveness and/or his loyalty. Unfortunately, girls have a hard time believing a guy who doesn't ask for sex is doing so just because he loves the girl too much to jeopardize her future.

One girl even said to me, "Even though I didn't want to have sex, I at least wanted him to ask." Why did she want him to ask? Because she wanted to know she was desirable. Girls want guys to like them enough to want to have sex with them but love them enough to refrain. Do you see how confusing this can be for guys? I understand girls wanting to feel desirable. It's unfortunate a request for sex is their measuring stick. If a guy is attracted to you, he'll show it in the way he treats you, not just by asking for sex.

Assumption 3: Something is better than nothing.

I spoke with a senior football player after class one day. He told me he dated a girl who said she didn't want to have sex until she had graduated from college. He respected and accepted her decision.

Unfortunately, the girl wanted to do everything but have sex. He said he had done everything but "stick it in," and she was the one who initiated everything. He broke up with her because even though she could get that close to sex and stop, it was too difficult for him to do so. He said they *may* have dated longer if they hadn't done anything as opposed to her "teasing" him.

Some girls believe guys will get bored with them if they aren't doing something. So they try to get as close to sex as possible without actually having sex. Again, this goes back to girls feeling as if their first priority is to please a guy to keep him. Once a girl begins down the path of pleasing a guy, he'll want as much as he can get. She thinks if she gives him X, she can satisfy him. What she doesn't realize is she's just gotten him to the point where he wants more.

Young ladies, once guys have been sexually stimulated, they want to be sexually satisfied. In fact, if they do get aroused and aren't satisfied, it can be painful and aggravating for them. As a result, many guys tell me they would rather you not stimulate them if they can't go all the way.

Why don't girls wait for sex?

Young men now tell me they're having a hard time finding young ladies who will wait for sex.

> *"Thank you for confirming I have made the correct choice in choosing to be a virgin. I found out many girls do not appreciate my views, and for a while I even doubted my decision because of it. Since your talk, I am now firm in my decision again, and I hope I can find a girl who respects my views."*
>
> —High School Guy

> *"I miss the image of girls with values my mother always drilled into my head, but I never see them around me."*
>
> —High School Guy

> "I'm waiting for the day I meet a girl that respects herself enough to not have sex. Those are the keepers."
>
> ~ HIGH SCHOOL GUY

Many girls do choose to wait for sex, but some girls are also initiating the sex. I believe there are several underlying reasons why they do so.

1 Girls think their boyfriends will have sex with someone else.

A lot of girls tell me, "The reason I had sex with my boyfriend is because I was afraid I might lose a boyfriend I really like." I always respond, "Losing him is definitely a possibility. You may lose a boyfriend you like, but you'll never lose a boyfriend who really likes you." Think about it, young ladies: If a guy really likes you, I don't care how high your standards are, he'll break his neck trying to meet them.

> *If a guy really likes you, I don't care how high your standards are, he'll break his neck trying to meet them.*

If a guy wants to be with you long term, he will do whatever it takes to be with you, including waiting. He would be willing to do that and anything else you ask of him.

> "I've been in a relationship for a year, and I'm in love with her. When I first met her everything changed, and I mean everything . . . I always knew I was working for something, and you helped me see that. She set a bar I'm

working to reach. She is still a virgin, and I'm planning to prove to her sex doesn't matter to me, only her love does."

~ High School Guy

The truth of the matter is more guys would abstain from sex if more girls demanded it. They wouldn't have a choice. But, let's face it, for every girl who refuses to have sex with a guy, there are probably five or ten others who will be more than willing to give him what he wants. And unfortunately, the girls who want to abstain are afraid to lose their boyfriend to one of the girls who will have sex with him. But what does a girl lose if a guy leaves just because he didn't get sex? Not much.

If all girls could get together and make a pact to demand respect from guys, I think we would see a different reality. Girls really do have the power to change the culture when it comes to sex.

"The fact that many of us have degraded ourselves tells us the problem isn't just with males, but with ourselves. Men just realized what was happening and took advantage of it. We are part of the problem, so we must be part of the solution. If men see we have elevated our standards, they'll have no choice but to elevate their own."

~ High School Girl

2 Girls give up too soon and settle.

Girls don't think they can get what they want, so they settle for what they can get.

"I wish I would have heard you speak a long time ago. I've made many mistakes in my past, and I'm just now seeing how bad my choices have hurt me. I've changed and learned to respect myself and learned sex doesn't bring love or commitment. A year ago I met my boyfriend. It was love at first sight. When we got to know each other, I learned he was still a virgin and I'm not. He said he was waiting for the right one. We struggle a lot with my past choices and how they affect him. If I knew I'd find true love one day, I would have waited a million years. It's hard, and I always wish I would have done things differently."

— HIGH SCHOOL GIRL

> *Girls don't think they can get what they want, so they settle for what they can get.*

Often, girls are so desperate to have a boyfriend they settle for the first boy who shows interest. Just because a guy likes you doesn't mean he's right for you. But let's be honest, most girls haven't even thought about what makes a guy "right" for them, beyond the physical characteristics.

I recently spoke to a young lady after class. She was dating someone even her closest friends couldn't understand why she would be with him. They knew he always got in trouble in school, was cocky and treated girls badly. When I asked why she was dating him, she said, "Because he asked." She also indicated she planned to have sex with him the following weekend. Again, just because he asked. Apparently, she had a low standard because she made her decisions just because he asked. In fact, I wouldn't even call this a standard at all. I'm sure he may have been good-looking, which may have been all she needed to date him.

Here's a scenario that plays out all too often:

A girl feels left out because all her friends have boyfriends and she doesn't. This makes her question her attractiveness. So she spends a great deal of her time trying to figure out what she can do to get a guy to like her. She may change her wardrobe and wear more revealing clothes just to catch a guy's eye.

Even though sex isn't something she plans on doing or wants to do, she thinks she may have to do it if she wants to have a boyfriend. That's what all guys want. After all, sex is just a normal part of a relationship, right? Not to mention, most of her friends have already had sex, or so they say, so what would be the big deal?

The first guy who shows an interest in her and asks her to be his girlfriend gets a "yes." She hopes the relationship lasts "a long time." But even if it doesn't, at least she can now say she's had a boyfriend and stop feeling like such a loser.

> *You may be just one boyfriend away from the one who will recognize your worth and wait for you.*

When he asks her to have sex, she knows it's probably not a good idea. She may even decline at first. She offers to do other things with/for him, hoping she can please him without taking that big step. He keeps begging her to go all the way. She gets tired of him asking, and he wears her down. She's afraid if she doesn't do it, he might get upset with her, so she gives in. She may even feel like she's supposed to do whatever he wants as repayment for him making her his girlfriend.

Before she had sex with him, she didn't give any thought to what would happen after they had sex that first time. She didn't realize he was going to expect her to continue having sex, making her feel guilty if she doesn't. So she continues doing it. Even when things get rocky with the relationship, she hangs on. She doesn't want to lose the guy she trusted with her body. Despite all her best efforts, the relationship ends, and she's devastated.

She thought sex was the only way to keep a relationship. But she didn't realize that maybe the next guy she dated would have been the one who was willing to wait. She just gave up too soon because she was so desperate to have a boyfriend. You may be just one boyfriend away from the one who will recognize your worth and wait for you. Whatever you do, don't settle and give up too soon.

This young lady also didn't realize another important fact. It's something I never want you to forget:

You are the prize.

You should be the one who gets to decide whether you like him enough to be with him instead of hoping he likes you. Does he deserve to be with you? If you don't understand this, you will spend the rest of your life trying to measure up to someone else's standards instead of finding someone who measures up to yours. But, to do this, you have to set standards. You also have to know your value.

It's a lot less work to figure out what you want and determine whether a guy meets your standards than to try to figure out what the guy wants and spend all your time and energy trying to win him over. Just be yourself—you can never go wrong when you are.

Just be yourself—you can never go wrong when you are.

"It's sad some girls have sex to feel liked, not because they like it. I'm a guy, and I will tell you any girls that *think they need to look a certain way for us to like them are wrong. We like you for who you are. I just wish girls would be themselves and understand they're pretty that way."*

—High School Guy

3 She thinks she's responsible for guys' happiness.

Girls think making a guy happy is what a good girlfriend is supposed to do.

"My boyfriend kept pressuring me to have sex, and I kept refusing. He wouldn't stop insisting until one day I finally caved in. It wasn't because I wanted to, but it was for him to be happy, which finally cost me my happiness. Ever since I had sex, I haven't been able to be happy like I was before."

—High School Girl

> A guy's happiness is not a girl's responsibility.

Young ladies, I wish I could hang this banner in the sky: A guy's happiness is not a girl's responsibility.

You must understand if you haven't decided what makes you happy, where your boundaries are or what your standards and values are (independent of a relationship), you will spend the rest of your life like a puppet on a string. This boyfriend wanted you to do this, so you did it. The next boyfriend wanted you to do that, so you did it. And before long, you wake up one day and you don't even recognize the person you have become.

> "Your words opened my eyes. When you spoke of one of the situations, it made me cry. It was like you told my story without letting everyone know. I wish you had come earlier in my life. You would have made an impact on the choices I made back then. Being sexually active has changed my life. I am known for doing something I know the real me would have never done. Now I feel like I lost myself completely, and I'm still trying to find myself today."
>
> — HIGH SCHOOL GIRL

It's hard to know who you are if you spend your life becoming the person each boyfriend wants you to be.

Young ladies, no relationship is worth losing yourself over. Who you are is good enough. And anyone who doesn't appreciate you the way you are doesn't deserve you.

It's bad enough girls are willing to have sex with guys just because they asked and girls will do anything to make them happy. I'm now finding girls who are offering to have sex with guys because they assume that will make him happy. Guys don't even have to ask for it.

A few years ago, a young man approached me after the second day of hearing me speak to his class to ask for my advice. He was a high school junior.

His girlfriend was a sophomore, who originally told him she wanted to wait until marriage for sex. Recently she told him she changed her mind and now wanted to have sex with him on prom night. He said now he didn't know what to do because he lost all respect for her when she changed her mind about sex. He said, "One of the things I respected about her the most was that she had standards and wanted to wait until marriage for sex. Now she's telling me something different, and I'm not sure what to do about that. I don't respect her anymore. What should I do?"

My response to him: "I like to give everyone the benefit of the doubt. She did not have the opportunity to hear what you heard over the past couple of days. If she had heard the same presentation you heard, maybe she wouldn't have changed her mind about when she wanted to have sex. I would go back to her and share everything you heard during my class and see if she still wants to have sex on prom night. If she does, then maybe she's not the right girl for you."

A couple of weeks later, I saw the young man in the hall when I returned to the school to teach other classes. I asked him how the conversation went with his girlfriend. He told me they broke up because he couldn't stay with her after she changed her mind about sex.

I'm sure the young lady thought her boyfriend would be elated when he found out she was willing to have sex with him on prom night. She may have thought to herself, *He is going to be so happy when I tell him I have a little something special for him on prom night if he sticks around until the spring.* Instead, she lost what could have been a long-term relationship because sex wasn't what he wanted. Offering sex may not have even been what the young lady wanted to do. It may have just been what she thought she had to do to keep him around and make him happy.

What are the benefits of waiting?

When I talk about sex with students, I like to teach toward something instead of away from something. I'd much rather spend my time discussing the benefits of abstaining from sex than the consequences of having sex. Below is one of my favorite stories that shows the benefits of choosing to wait for sex.

> **CASE STUDY**
> *Tony and Julie*
>
> This is a story of two of my good friends, Tony and Julie. When they met they were both twenty-four years old. Julie was a virgin and Tony wasn't. Check out this conversation I had with Tony to see how their relationship evolved.
>
> **Tony:** When we first started dating, Julie told me she was a virgin. She also said she wouldn't be having sex with me or anyone else until her wedding night.
>
> **Me:** I love the fact that she knew her value. So she basically said, 'This is my price. You can either pay this price or you can keep stepping and I'll wait for someone who will.' I wish more girls were this confident.
>
> **Tony:** If I had met her in high school or college, that's exactly what I would have done—kept stepping. At that time, I wasn't looking for 'Mrs. Right.' I was looking for 'Ms. Right Now.' But at twenty-four years old, knowing she was a virgin was very

attractive to me. Her value in my eyes went up. *[Anything that's rare is automatically worth more.]* We dated for a year before we got engaged, and we were engaged for a year. We had sex for the first time on our wedding night.

Me: Wow. Most girls don't think any guy would wait, especially not two years.

Tony: I'm glad Julie raised the standard and required me to marry her before having sex. She showed me how much self-control I had. The same self-control it took for me to not have sex with Julie while we were dating is the same self-control it takes for me not to cheat on her now that we're married. I have more women hitting on me with a ring on my finger than I ever did without.

Me: Oh my goodness. That's exactly what I tell the students—you don't get discipline and self-control as a wedding gift. If you don't have self-control before you get married, saying two words—"I Do"—will not give you the self-control you will need to stay faithful to your spouse.

Discipline truly is the key to success. If you can show self-control in the key area of sex, it will pay huge dividends in every other area of your life. This area will be the most difficult for you to have discipline in because this is a natural desire. If you have discipline when it comes to sex, the sky is the limit as far as how successful you will be in life. You will have mastered the most difficult thing in your life, yourself.

> I spoke with Tony again, and he provided more information about his decision.
>
> **Tony:** Here's something else you can share with your students. Abstaining from sex is a great way to determine how strong you are. I had no idea I was that strong. If one of my buddies had come to me a month before I met Julie and told me I would ever go two years without sex, I would have told him he was crazy. I'll always appreciate Julie for helping me see my true strength.

Some people will never know their true strength because they don't challenge themselves. It's easy to say you have the discipline and self-control to abstain from sex. The only way to prove it is with your actions. As a matter of fact, a sexually active sixteen-year-old guy once told me, "I don't have to have sex. I just like it, but I don't have to have it. I can go without it if I wanted to because I have self-control. I just don't want to because I like it. But I don't have to have it." I finally asked him if he was trying to convince himself or me. I told him if he didn't have to have it, he should prove it. He didn't need to prove it to me. He should prove it to himself because until he didn't have sex, those were just words anyone could say.

Let's get back to Tony and Julie. I shared their story with a male friend. He said, "Any man who would deny his urges,

> *Some people will never know their true strength because they don't challenge themselves.*

hormones and flesh for two years to be with a woman is a man that won't give up on his marriage easily. He has invested too much 'skin in the game.'" Tony and Julie have been happily married for twenty-five years. Tony travels across the country with his job. Do you think Julie is sitting at home wondering if he's cheating on her while he's on the road? I doubt it! He proved to her before they got married that he had self-control, so the trust level is only higher now that they're married.

> "When you give up something now for something better later, that's not a sacrifice. That's an investment."
>
> ~ ANDY STANLEY, Pastor of North Point Community Church

Tony and Julie were willing to abstain from sex while they were dating. Why? To build a firm foundation for a marriage that would stand the test of time. Are you willing to invest in your future marriage and family? Are you willing to not do some things sexually while you are dating to increase the chances of having a successful marriage? Sadly, all too often, I see the opposite happening. I see young people making decisions during their teenage dating years that will decrease their chances of getting what they say they want when they become an adult, like the young lady below.

> "I lost my virginity to a guy I thought I loved. After a while I felt sick, and knew I was with child, but I didn't want to believe it. When I told him, all he said was, 'Get rid of it. I'm too young.' My heart broke. I didn't kill it, but I gave it to a good family. I was hurt for so long, and all I ever thought was he loved me, but he didn't love me. He loved my body and the fact that he was my only . . .

I will never trust another man, which is why I don't love or care anymore."

— HIGH SCHOOL GIRL

This is a prime example of a young lady who may have jeopardized her chance to have a healthy marriage because of a choice she made in a temporary relationship. She says she will never trust another guy again, which I hope is not true. If it is true, then she'll go into a marriage relationship with trust issues, if she gets married at all. Her future may have looked a lot different if she had not had sex with a guy who ended up being just an ex-boyfriend.

So, let's summarize some of the benefits of abstaining from sex:

1. It develops the discipline and self-control that will also be necessary for success in life and once you're married.
2. It decreases your chances of taking physical and emotional baggage into your marriage.
3. It builds your relationship on a solid foundation that is not physical.

Now that you know...

Guys would wait to have sex much more often than they do if adult male role models, the media, society and even girls didn't put so much pressure on them to have sex. If you were to ask sexually active guys how many of them really wanted to have sex, half of them would probably tell you they didn't feel they had a choice. They often feel pressured into it just like girls do. Many of them are trying to figure out how to be a man, and unfortunately what they see and hear leads them to believe having sex is the measure of manhood.

Yes, there are plenty of guys who will use girls to satisfy their hormones at any and every chance they get, but I don't want you to put all guys in that category because many guys prefer quality to quantity. Quality guys are looking for quality girls. So instead of spending your time trying to please the guys who prefer quantity, you would be better off focusing on becoming a quality girl. Quality girls respect and protect themselves and don't accept less from their partners. When the quality guy who doesn't want sex and would love you for you shows up, you two will be perfect for each other.

> *"Are you the person that the person you are looking for is looking for?"*
>
> ~ ANDY STANLEY, Pastor of North Point Community Church

There is nothing more attractive to a guy than a quality girl who has standards, loves herself, knows where she wants to go in life and is focusing her efforts on getting there. When a guy finds a girl like this, he will do whatever it takes to be with her, including abstaining from sex.

> *"I have a girlfriend of thirteen months, and when you mentioned if you love someone you keep their best interest at heart, it spoke to me. This is because I feel as if I do love her and I have never pressured her into sex because I know where she places her standards, and I don't think there is anything more attractive than*

they will wait if you will

that. And she is the only girl I have imagined having a future with, and because of your talks I have a better understanding of what is most important, and that is her, not parts of her."

～ HIGH SCHOOL GUY

This is the kind of guy you deserve. Please don't settle for less.

Conclusion

So what have we learned?

1. Sex doesn't equal love, despite what guys and movies may tell you.
2. Guys will tell you what you want to hear to get what they want. It's the oldest trick in the book.
3. Guys won't respect you if you don't respect yourself, so know your value and don't settle for less.
4. Sex changes things—and normally not for the better.
5. Guys are not looking for a wife, no matter how much you think he's the one.
6. They can't replace your father—no matter how hard they try.
7. Guys will wait if you will, so keep your standards high.

It may seem logical after reading this book that sex as a teenager doesn't make sense. You may even think it'll be easy to abstain. But, will it be easy six, twelve, eighteen months from now after what you read in this book is no longer fresh in your mind? It's easy to say you're not going to have sex when you're not in a relationship. It'll be a lot more difficult when you get in one.

You may even be willing to commit to waiting to have sex until you are in a long-term, committed mutually monogamous relationship (a.k.a. marriage). The only way you can make this

conclusion

commitment and have any chance of keeping your commitment is by setting boundaries. You need boundaries in three areas: people, places and physical boundaries.

> **People boundaries:** Decide who you will date and who your friends will be. If you don't want to have sex and you're dating someone who does, you are only making it difficult on yourself. Also, if the majority of your friends are sexually active, you may feel pressure to have sex so you're not left out of conversations when they're talking about what they're doing with their boyfriends.
>
> **Places boundaries:** Decide where you will go while you're on your date. If you're not trying to have sex, you should avoid those places where it can happen.
>
> **Physical boundaries:** Decide how far is too far. The biggest mistake people make when it comes to sex is, believing they'll be able to stop things after they get started and before things go too far. The time to show self-control is before things get heated, not after.

No one makes it through life without boundaries. Just remember boundaries are there to protect you, not to limit your fun. The sooner you can set and maintain them, the better.

Now that you know, I hope you'll keep these secrets in mind when making decisions about love, sex and relationships. I wrote this book for girls just like you because I believe your health and future are priceless. Nothing should keep you from achieving your full potential. I have faith that once armed with the real truth, you won't accept less than you deserve.

WHAT KIND OF GUY DO YOU HAVE?

No need to wonder with this must-have cheat sheet that breaks down the three types of guys and how the 7 secrets apply to each one.

Download this cheat sheet NOW by going to:

www.7secretsofguys.com/cheatsheet